'He Lives In A Parallel Universe'

Sunny Jetsun

'He Lives In A Parallel Universe'

Sunny Jetsun

This book is arranged from 'Surreal' notes made from Inspired conversations with friends during the 2010/2011 winter season in Anjuna, Goa "Thank you all" Happy 2012. Om Shanti Shanti

Originally Published as Sunny Jetsun
'Driving My Scooter Through The Asteroid Field
Coming Down Over Venus ~ "Hallo Baba"
'Light love Angels from Heaven. New Generation,
Inspiration, Revolution, Revelation ~
All the Colours of Cosmic Rainbows'
*'Green Eve * Don't lose the Light Vortex **
My brain's gone on holiday ~ free flowing feelings'
'Surfing or Suffering ~ together * Sense Consciousness
fields of a body with streams and stars of hearts'
"When You're happy you got wings on your back ~
Reposez vos oreilles a Goa; We're only one kiss away"
'PSYCHIC PSYCHEDELIC'
'Streaming Lemon Topaz Sunbeams'
'Invasion of Beauty *FLASH * The Love Mudras'
'Patchouli Showers ~ Tantric Temples'
'It's Just a Story ~ We Are All The Sun, Sweet Surrender'
Anthology #1 ~ 'Enjoy The Revolution'
Anthology # 2 ~ 'Love & Freedom ~ Welcome'
'Queen of Space ~ King of Flower Power ~ dripping Rainbows'
'All Love Frequency ~ In Zero Space'
Peace Goddess*Spirit of the Field*The Intimacy Sutras

'Heavenly Bodies ~ Celestial Alignments*
Feeling ~ Energy that Is LOVE in Itself'
'I've been to Venus & back*These Are Real Feelings*
Let the Universe Guide Your Heart*through Space'
* The Kiss In Slaughterhouse 6 *

Books by the Same Author:

Originally Published as Ciel Rose
'Sadhu Sadhu Sadhu ~ "All Beings Be Happy" ~ Shanti Shanti'
'Trilogy Of Vibrations ~ The Oneness Of Life'
'Each Fragment of Life Is Sacred ~ These Are Your Children'
'Young Women Spin On Their Doorsteps At Dusk'
'Life Is Simple, Sharing ~ Loving Kindness From The Heart'
'The Universe Coming Across The River'

Originally Published as Sunny Revareva
'Pure Light ~ Cosmic * Sweet Heart ~ We've All Got Stars Inside'
'Perfect Love ~ No Mind * Star Light ~ Come Alive'
'True Freedom ~ Natural Spiritual Beauty ~
Here * Now ~ Gems of Eternity'

Sunny Jetsun Online at:
Website: www.sunnyjetsun.com
Facebook: www.facebook.com/sunnyjetsun
Amazon: www.amazon.com/author/sunnyjetsun

Flower Is Life

Are you a Mayan Toker? ~ "¼ a day keeps the Doctor away"
I like Extra Hot too ~ that's what it taught me ~ just to let go.
'A body full of steroids & a pocket full of Coke!' El Caliente!
"I was comin' at you" be less fake, be your self ~
'Flipped my brain on its head ~ flipped in'
Freaks at the Acid party wearing amazing fancy dress masks.
Coconut meteorites landing on your roof.
Keep back & smile.

12* Geisha Balls

"If I can do it anybody can do it!" A belief is only a thought
that you think. So let's have it as a belief to manifest creation.
Get a wetsuit jump in ~ Splish Splash! BlissSSS State Feeling
In a dark room for sure you need a light" for the impending ~
Holding up all the Identities, parameters of the Conditionings.
Holding on to it without ever letting go to take your next step.
We're all Occupied, got us by the nuts, Karma Bride override.
Just testing your Stress Levels Baba, in a room full of Spiders!
Let's have Kinetic Sculpture ~ full Ecstatic dance in the waves.

All in the End

God made Hell there's a reason otherwise why did he make Hell?
How other energies grab you, not just another wave ~ Nothing
left for the Mind to grip; Allow them to melt into other realities.
She could understand the birds, over the wind, in every channel.
We decided to ignore all the contradictions, dualities of reality.
Consciously see how we can be ~ Loving that and adoring her.
LSD ~ Did you benefit from it emotionally, lost your migraine?
The Tantric Guru dodging the drips ~
Eternal process ~ can't wait for anything.
We're Open ~ energising Mind through awareness.
We're always lookin' there, can't see what's here!
Fireflies being in the eternal with telepathic angels

1

Unexpected Super Tel E pathic L S D Aci*dose*i*us

I don't know anything ~ She's gorgeous & Super natural.
Apparently they're from an eccentric, dysfunctional family.
"Who would have thought!" Enjoying the freedom of the thrill.
Funtastic that one night stand, loving it with a Perfect stranger.
Perfect breasts, perfect kisses, smiling ~ sucking in the moment!
Came home she got naked, full power carnal knowledge surprise.
At dawn she took a taxi for her flight to somewhere in Ukrainia.

'Money is a Great Motivator'

When I realized it, I got a shock!
Bloodsucking the people's wealth.
Keeping them Interested in Debt ~
to someone; Who makes the Control?
International financial lenders, Predators!
"Let the pain flow out and give it to the Divine"
Awareness of any forgiveness.

Sold for a Copper Pan

Do you ever feel like burning ~ going up in crazy, hazy smoke?
In a Love bubble, not saving anybody; I'm saving myself Baba.
That's why it's the Holy Ghost ~ "I've never Idolised anything.
When you buy & Sell People, burning cars on the street's nout!
Want it Spontaneous right now right here. She's my Love child.
Just gettin' on with it, walked around the corner & WOW!
Rammed with totty

You're the ONE

What Idea do you want? Looking out for it.
You can live it the way you want to live ~
"Compromise is the lie of not being myself"
"I've got to see it, feel it to believe it"
"She wasn't demonic enough!"
'In a Death by drugs room 1200 Rupees'

Ultra*Charismatic
"We're on the other side of the lead cataclysmic wheel"
"Didn't see anything I was enjoying, down at the beach"
"Do you know a place called the Ding Dong in Aswem?"
That's flipping your brain like everyone, I need my fix!
Girl's sexy skin tight mini string in a tropical paradise.
That's the attraction of girls isn't it? Primal Magnets ~
I just sucked it right in magically down the Cosmic river
through a Supra naturalism of Sensual Pleasure

'Total Violence & Total Opening Potential'
Star Trek, X Files, The Simpsons, & Fritz the Cat on Peyote,
testing every thing in his van along the Super Highway of Life.
84 and frightened to Open the door ~ obsessed, brainwashed,
Compulsion. 70 years old and you're dead before you're dead'
Turn on the TV; go to your favourite Vampire, Horror channel
Someone will understand it ~"What people don't understand is
we're All violent inside!" Who's got their hands on the Remote?

Good for Suffering
Get the Pain Killers out!
"Light the Fire, get on with it!"
You can see why people walk around mountains on their knees?
"Not really"

Nod & Smile of Density!
"Somebody should break her heart so she feels what it is like!"
Puppets reading the News; The Truth happens; It is happening
New Satellites launched into the sky ~ to see cosmic rain fall.
Bring in those transgendered Christians to meet the Gladiators!
What sort of Mindset is that? Globalism, Oligarchy & Tyranny!
Let's be delirious, we're all human beings living in a biosphere.
This is Not a dream ~ turning rain into rainbows not Monsters!

'Tete a Tete'

Fondling bevies of Gopis, swooning in a soft languid breeze.
"At this moment I want a lot of women to play with"
Valuable in the reflection ~ how long for your Purdah?
8 Chakra Baba going to the fountain at the Holy Mountain.
'We need a million Tantric temples like this around the World'
"Don't Open your mouth until I tell you" ~ "Here's a drop!"
Live in the moment ~ You can only decide for Your self.
"Don't believe anything anyone tells You"
Engorged Psychedelic Clitorises ~ Go & find out for yourself.
Drop All Labels, no answers to be found unless you want one.
Unraveling, revealing, In/divi/dual process of your own Quality.
A matter of Understanding, eating that soup; What we cook ~
we have to eat now and get up from the table when it's empty.

Going to the Glowing Source
Surrounded by people living in the happy vibe ~
Push value out and let it flow ~ living with my tribe.
We all want something more ~ until!
Wherever you got that feeling in your heart
Life continues ~

She has to break the Illusion Mould but It's Alive In My Mind!
Hyper active, ADHD; You understand her. I think I understand.
Myself sorry can't be involved in your crazy world; Channelin'
He means it, I Love it, now you Know; We've all done that one.
She told me stories, her sexy toys, catamite boys, she don't lie!
I'm falling in Love with you, Open, letting our energies attract,
black, white, Yellow, blue, red it's all inclusive, Unconditional.
Look at our behavior Cleopatra, Maniacs Insanities, brutalities.
Tyrannical despots, decadent psychopaths, no respect for life!
Selfless, Unconditional Love pitted against Licentious evils.
Always like to see the good guys in action ~ Trusting to Trust

<u>Paradise Now</u>
Good Life ~ "I haven't got time to come down"
"Are you gonna move it for her?" "I'll lift one end"
Take responsibility, You have to 'Own It'; It's being Conscious,
choices you make with your Karma; Where you takin' me now?
One burst of energy going in 5 different ways ~
Chasing my thoughts on a rollercoaster.
"I came in as the Lover"

<u>In Another Frequence.</u>
Dragons are another expression of Mother Earth.
Like us and transmuting ~ Fire, light puts you higher.
Utopian Intent ~ can be your Reality just be in the moment.
How does it feel being in the ZERO of allowance? Gives Space
for Spirit to Unfold ~ whatever it will be ~ differently, infinity.
In a Playground where the dualities are forming in the friction.
Expression of your Qualities, what do you want to show?
Making a Higher expression ~ Cosmic Consciousness

<u>"It's My Body ~ It's My Temple"</u>
It's all a game. I phoned the DSS from Baga beach.
They said, "You haven't been for your Medicals!"
Others Just looting and robbing, Mindless violence!
Freedom Openness, Not our capitalist Government's ideology!
Yeah we're all Philosophers ~ getting Bad Advice for Wonga.
Behind their masks a bunch of pretentious, arrogant fascists!
"Thank God for the Miniskirt and to girls for wearing them!"
Whoever wants to wear a black nylon sheet in 100* can do so!
A Chastity belt it's all about Possession of the Women by Men.
Anaemic, they're hiding their juicy bits ~"I Own My Treasure"
Kicked to other side of the Universe, Star portal, on a one way ticket.
"You going to the Next Level or not?"
Caressing a Sweet Ankh*let

Crust of Crystals
Enjoying Mother Earth as soon as you leave the Highway.
You're off the Grid. Out of the loop ~ nature's not a Matrix.
Over powering Isolation ~ standing in your own shiny shoes!
Smoking for Shiva, loves you to smoke, have the best experience.
"The days are filled because you don't put anything special in"
What the fuck was that! I've given up on it ~ I've accepted it.
It's gone, not a worry anymore, dispelled the deep karmic seed.
"We used to play round Bomb shelters in Anti Personal Craters"

Sacred Bio. Ceremonies
Encountered baby Beelzebub with an AK47! 'Hippy Killer'
Dead famous, cutting corners in India ~ A right Fakir bodge!
One puff ~ to another world, feed the weed Ayuhuascan Pilot!
Taking the edge off it ~ making the Square mile into a Circle!
"You have to give it total respect, the less class A's the better."
Twisted, hot & curious flowering inside a cave full of enzymes.
"When I die my eyes will be closed, my heart will be Open"
'Hard Life Well Lived' ~ ask the Punk Hottentot Venus.

The Baba's Shop
He's a friend, he knows many people, lost in the Pubic triangle.
"Your wife is a whore in my Palace." That's a Tough one!
Goddess of the Vagina carved into my diamond lotus locket.
"I'm comin' through don't get in me way or I'll mince you!"
All yu wanna do is live the life yu wanna live ~ while
they worked on putting out the negative Frequency ~
False Identifications ~ go in that state & ask for Help!
Have the allowance to let it be ~ to give up to it.
Angels are Vibrations that you call in ~
letting them through to give us the light.
Your Intent becomes Reality ~
She's healing my Soul.

'Catherine Wheel'
Holding the frequency, no Judgment, calling the Angels.
We are light beings ~ shifting in Astral bliss Consciousness.
Higher intensity, speed, Allowance from our heart to create ~
Wisdom of the Mind in a 'Cosmic field of Order ~ Lemon cake'
Letting go not doing, allowing that higher vibration to take over
I'm traveling on my journey of discovery of my self absolutely!

Orgonite Bonging
Just want the Binggggggggg bang ~ have to stay in the fire
of transmutation ~ otherwise it will hang on you like shit....
Going through elemental fire doing it for the best of everyone.
Do it more on a Love Level ~ No more Polarities in our Crystal.
Sitting in the Violet flame purer angels resonating much higher
through the laser of the Mind ~ through it not dependent on it.
Darshan Download ~ falling in the reflective Pools of Infinity.
Bringing it together... 'In Lak ech', "Hallo, Namaste!"

Bliss Beach
Anjuna, Goa, India, 'The Hippie Mecca'
Feeling the Harmony and Peace at the Hanuman Temple.
Sitting in Nirvana gazing at the wonder of the Himalayas.
Psychedelic, exotic beauties swimming in the sea of Siam.
Connecting the harmony in the here & now presence.
Trusting your own feelings ~
You are always in Paradise.

'The Lie'
I create my own Reality ~ how you see it.
You can Relax in it ~ feel its resonance.
See how it flows by Itself ~ thru duality.
Allowing the flow to be ~
Delusion that we are separated
FROM IT

Helios ~ Sun Sultan
Obelisks of Amun, Karnak to the Oceanic Pyramid at Tulum.
Rendez vous by a Megalith with the famed 7 dolls of Oxkintok.
Anunnaki arriving from the 6th Planet
Passed the 8 Rayed star of Venus
saw Jacob wrestling an Angel ~
Took the 'Ben Ben' Celestial boat and met Ra
on her way from Jupiter to Earth ~ Terra firma.

'Kallisti' ~ The Beautiful Island.
Astral Messages at a Ziggurat of the Red Jaguar, Chichen Itza.
Met Invaders of the Toltecs solving an enigmatic Mystic cube,
deciphering Legends of Atlantis vibrating inside Phaestos' tube.
Rejecting harmful 'anti psychotic' drugs, many Chemical Koshes!
Climbed to the apex of Quetzal's Temple with my hot Phoenician
Trance bride, her sparkly eyes singing Love, Peace, Rock & Roll ~
don't be long!

'Chasing Medieval Flames'
Humanitarian of the 1st order left in the cemetery of the Kings.
Site was Catastrophic, Bombs screaming into the Green Zone!
Hot load into an Evacuation helicopter, traumatized in twilight.
"God made men ~ Men made slaves"

My Thing
'This Big Connection with Nature!
Need Agreed Not Greed ~ Quality of Life for us all.

Energy Field Paintings
Contemplation of the reality of their latest discovery
of No Mind ~ living in a World of apparent Insanity!
Made another bloody sacrifice to his Gods of duality.
The Deity was enticed by the smell of roasting meat.
How about that? There you go then, in a mad Frenzy!

Le Sensorial Imagination ~ Enchantment & Inspiration.
Who Am I; A Human? Was he taking any Psyche active drugs?
Yes something Original; Taking a tablet of 360* for the Brain!
Observing the Sub Conscious ~ Art showing Separate Realities
Your Self ~ seeing through Mirrors of Dream, Multi Identities.
Flying over snowy mountain peaks. Dancing with a green fairy.
Dreaming of an Aryan Goddess, beautiful naked female Queen.
Holding Sky bird cut - outs filled with azul space and reveries.
Mystic Owls flying through Landscapes of the Mind's symbols.
Green apples, celestial nymphs, silhouettes, bowler hats, pipes,
abstract rainbows, silver spheres of Suprasense Consciousness.
Smiling to myself; Searching for Truth, on a bright, sunny day.
White clouds drifting over the calm, languid, aquamarine sea.
Feelings of Intuition, evoking ~ light beyond some far horizon.

*

Are these Representations Hallucinations, illusions, delusions?
Passing along cold, dark tunnel walls, by a grey stone balcony.
Framing a view into the Surreal distance out beyond ~ Infinity.
Aware of more energy fields becoming manifested! Spirituality.
Surprise, pictures unfolding ~ Tarot of Psychology & Prophecy.
'The Great Expectation, La Memoire, La Faith, Boundlessness.
Standing in a Circle of Clairvoyance, embracing a magic fish.
Visual language, Poetry, codes, hieroglyphics of the Irrational
understanding, not making any normal, formal sense of reality.
Psychedelic Mind playing in Creation ~ Extra Dimensionality.
'Memory' of a Voyage, the blank page suspending a full moon,
looking at distant houses, windows illuminated in the Twilight.
Heart wearing a violet mask interpreting spatial Timelessness.
All Paradox out of Context. Question, does it make you Think?
Searching for the Empire of the Absolute in a Gothic hologram.
Eggs in a nest, bright stars' reflections in a still pond at night.
Trees bare of leaves standing alone witness to passing seasons.
Is it a nightmare ~ it's a daydream, a trip into nature's Soul...

<u>Touching a Place to Dream</u>
Abstract Expressions, archetypes of Primal desires, revealing
Inner worlds of human and Universal truths, breaking through
the barriers identifying the mind. Caressing intuition sensually.
Evocation ~ "I was obliged to make a translation in the dark"
Disconnected the Psyche and put it in a picture, on the stage.
Met a hollow Therapeute, sat wearing his poncho & sombrero.
Framed inside him were white clouds floating in a full blue sky.
Asked myself again is he taking Psychetropics to see this vision?
His Inspiration of the deep 'Self' was painting inner Landscapes,
Hallucinatory, Psychological, Surreal, Imaginary, dreamscapes.
Metaphors for Psychedelic Daydreams of sub consciousness ~
Opening the windows, sailing to Infinity on a full moon Ocean.
Time to hatch a nestling egg ~ You've got my blessing.
Open to the feeling ~ of Conception with Love beams.

<u>Balance & Beauty</u>
Magical Acrobats juggling Crystal balls doing Bharata natyam
"World Class, something you'll not see the rest of your life!"
Go & say 'Hallo' Hula-hoop girl is amazing, a magic couple.
From the Temple of Dance ~ ethereal octaves dancing in the air.
Arti in the evenings, Shamans rowing boats across the Ganges.
Ultimately UNIQUE

<u>Alchemy Spark</u>
'Keep all the Gold' ~ Chakra on Cosmic fire.
'The dream is nice its reality is even better'
Making the concept Real ~ on the spiritual wave.
Supra Conscious ~ sub Conscious life forces.
"Got to get to the bottom of it" ~ "Fuck you
You gotta get to the Top of It!"
"There's a lot of Magic out there!"
Pure & Simple

10

<u>Steppenwolf Razzmatazz</u>
Met her and off to the Racetrack!
Romantics standing on a ley line ~
Cheering, "I really like your energy"
The best of American Rock & Roll
too much amazing Acid....

<u>Pop on the beach</u>
"Ding dong" "It wasn't mumbo-jumbo it was real inside ~
a confused, psychotic mind." What is the truth of a Vision?
Back brain, right hemisphere ~ full facial, shape recognition.
Imprinting encoded. Who are you, who am I? What do we see?
Woke up his world had changed ~ brain had a big movement!
Changed into something unrecognizable, everything else was
the same, had had a stroke; Memory suffering disorientation.
Interaction through recognising the expressions of an Identity.
Reformatted itself ~ One sense readapting for another sense.
Only way left was Communicating through touch.
One of their lads kept white rabbits in a cage.

<u>Everyone wants a Boost!</u>
The Movie is in you ~
How you look outside.
Everyone is going through
the intensity of change ~
New JOB description.
Work on the Inside ~
Recognize and do it.
Cleaning our crystal.
Everything else will fall apart ~
Focusing the density on the point.
What do you want to live, African Goddess?
Because it's changing all the time.
We are in its energetic array.

'Thoughts are Free' ~ as Free as money!
Who destroyed an Anti-fascist visionary, who belted the women?
Treated to the worst brutality in a new Nazi Concentration camp!
She did all that and ended up getting shot, he was tortured to bits!
Isolation, Kicked out his teeth, broke his legs, made him blind,
sent for Interrogation, beating the free thoughts out of his mind.
He kept his dignity to the end reading Rilke's poetry.
Who owns all this sin? 'Bye bye to humanity'

Corruption Eruption Decoy
Les droits humains, article 1:
'Wo/Men are born and remain free
and equal in rights' Hard to believe?
Using a sustainable natural resource ~
built it for the Montrose Lunatic Asylum.
Unearthed another Plan for Mass deception, reduction.
"Is this Real World or Exercise?" "No, this is Real World!"
Interceptor jets flew in the wrong direction ~ on an assumption
that the attack would come from the sea not from over the city!
"Now you can't Trust the official leaders of your Government!"
Civilian casualties should be down to a minimum Commander,
do you wish to deploy? "Let's nuke the bastards!" Praise be!
Abomination Bombin' here, Bombin' there, Bombin' everywhere!!

The Rishikesh Yogi Mafia
Free from the Mind trip ~ Mind always tellin' you what to do.
That is the ultimate dream machine ~ Happening according to
the Mind. Caught in the Maya ~ the Matrix. Flyin' on MDMA.
Be a nice person that's all. Stay in the beauty of it, stay in love.
Which Reality do you want? Red Pill or blue Pill or Rainbows?
Asking the Oracle on how to aspire to the Higher ~ bandwidth.
Intent making it happen ~ finding out the path and walking on it.
To just be in Eden

Intuitive*Yoga

A Major gateway with Magical numbers.
Met Hermit #9 making his own Universe.
Cleansing, relief, let it all go ~ release.
Making the Full Circle of Allowance
And Experiencing it ALL.
Becoming a Golden Pyramid.
Becoming Co Creators to it ~
Becoming a Crystal light being.

'Mother Gota Kola, Ka Maga'

"It's a blessing to leave the body"
Let the Universe take over reality.
Giving & receiving Compassion ~
Putting yourself in the Violet, golden white flame.
We think we have to be Separate to get more Power!
We live in Abundance, are you taking it for granted?
Welcome to Unified field*existence in the 5th Dimension.
You are Enlightened ~ just have to fall in its frequency
of enlightenment…You are it, embody it now

A Trillion Addicts

If you criminalise it you put it in a dark space ~
Small fishing villages smoking Heroin, brown sugar.
Quean showing deference to The Corporation of London.
Queen showing deference to a college of stony Roman Jesuits.
Sovereign Knights of Malta no territory but a big virtual State.
When you lose your Identifications with yourself; Try Rajma!
They're running the Show ~ Scooping up all the Rare Earth!
Black Pope is in Control of the White Pope. "God help us!"
Inhuman in their behaviour, beyond Ruthless! Best trick ~
Ruling it by telling the people that they are FREE and they
believe it!

Constructivism … (A G. Dixon, 'Art of Russia' BBC)
Comrade Makakovsky shot himself, alone sitting in his chair!
Denounced as a fantastic eccentric in a world of Social Realism.
Where is the absent, creative poet in the mould ~ of our pattern?
Add his name to 700,000 undesirables killed by Stalin's Police.
Heroic parachutists flying thru mosaic skies to save their State.
Soviet Angels defending the people from the exterminating Nazis
Avant Gardism, dissidents, all depicted living in a Happy Land!
Yes there's been an Imaginary Revolution, an even better Ideal.
'A painting of Uncle Joe, a holy Icon hanging on everyone's wall'
In the background a little black secret Police car; Watching You!
What do they do? "Let's have an underground Art Exhibition, da!"

Distractions ~ Holding Up the Energy
"I was a hippy before it became a dirty word" to some still it is.
Inspired like a Psychenaut to venture into the great unknown!
He asked me if I was a therapist ~ be in the frequency allowance
We basically stay in the now ~ now.
Coming closer to our own essence.

'In Sharing Is The Joy'
You see yourself in themselves ~
'Come back and engage with reality'
Giving ourselves to the Consciousness.
Through that we'll experience Jupiter's Power of abundance.
You realized how valuable, your own Freedom is.
You put it out there ~ someone picked it up.
Tempted but can't make a decision ~ Not tempted enough!
Guided by the Angels to you ~
Your aura ~ now ready to meet you.
Keep dreaming until you wake up!
Who needs a sexual partner for sustained sexual Tantric effort,
Enlightenment?

Clandestine Murderer

Smoking Guns, experts in an Infra Red field; High value Target.
Measuring his shadow, against angles of the sun, right next door.
In the name of National Security of the United States of America!
Putting on his Bomb vest. Drone spy in real time from 50,000ft.
Slaughtering their own animals, illiterate women and children.
Didn't want another martyr, burial consistent with Islamic Law
A digital trail, facial recognition ~ up linked to Forensics' data.
We got him! Inside Situation room, Number 1 guy on the Planet.
Child with a suicide belt will kill you just as quick, 'Charlie mike'
Muscle memory knows how to make missiles cruise in the dark.
Fire teams, let's go explosive, Black hawk down! Under Radar.
Perfect conditions for Stealth flying ~ Enforcer with a new skin.
A War Hero ~ Blasted to bits in Afghanistan! Brrrr Boooom!!
"We will smoke 'em out of their holes Pardner." Is it true?
Fresh eyes on a night without moonlight.
"Improve, Adapt, Overcome" 'Enemy Killed In Action'
Quintessential decisions ~
or another Elvis sighting!

They Are FREE

"Don't be stubborn! They're lights over Phoenix"
"There's a lot of traffic UP there and it's not ours!"
Bending Space with my Anti Matter machine ~
1000's of Psychedelic dainties ~ Time traveller.
Living in a box with the hope of winning a lottery jackpot!
I am DEPROGRAMMING ~ BEING HAPPY, my definition.
Christ Consciousness, You will never do harm to anyone again!
Co Creators for Pachimamba's ~ Teachings.
It's only you who makes it possible, happening ~
Transmuting it from Mother Earth to the 5th dimension.
Living in a beautiful lagoon with psychedelic mermaids.
Everyone is ONE.

Romantic Bossa Nova
Tatiana ~ "Let's get lost!"
Sita in the Cockpit singing
Sweet Samba Mantra.

Glamorized another Genocidal Husband, Top Dog Warmonger
Henry No 8; A Reformation of the church ala Chinese in Tibet!
"Is your Majesty considering another marriage, taking a wife?"
Transported to the Tower ala Caligula ala Hitler, Deformation!
Collateral Damage Excuse of all Sociopathic Tyrants & Despots
Just got rid of # 1-7 & acquired #8, until death wills us do part!
Please do not Insist ~ In a mind of Palace Intrigues and murder.
Pain of the fire extracting a confession of heresy by a paranoid
Inquisitor's infliction; Screaming tied to a scorching apple tree.
She received 10 lashes with a whip for driving alone in Jeddah.
"I wanted to see you smile" ~ You will go to Hell you beasts!
We are all subjects obeying the Royalty; On pain of death!
You know what happens to his Queens!

Raining People
Couple in Love with 200 others hit Ground Zero in 10 secs/Flat!
Loss & horror amplified the suffering! Went home with Trauma!
He was Killed by a falling body! 'Thud!'
"We have Hope because we have light" 'Whack!'
"What was left of the flying gentleman in his brown suit
after he landed on a Volkswagen beetle from the 111th floor?"
343 firemen went up in smoke…living consciously for the now.

The Sun Is Bliss
S/he is the Space for my secret ~
I don't mind ~ what's happening.
Forgot you are the subject, so distracted by the Object!
Allowing the in/divi/duality
You are the singularity

Killing the golden goose
Ministry of love is really the Ministry of War; Sure!
Predatory International money lenders on the loose.
Capital free traders wanting to make a Monopoly, Cartel.
It's never what it seems, what they want you to believe.
They love disaster movies in the USA; 24/7 pornography,
glamorous vampires of terror, a dedicated Horror channel,
violent psychopaths without empathy sit at every board meeting.
British Imperial, Shell, Halliburton, All Global Conglomerates.

Bombay Sausage Factory
"Let's go to the Amazon ~"
"I've seen it on the telly!"
You can cry on my shoulder.
"I just wanna wake up with someone who loves me"
Saying what you feel.

Insensitive ~ Sensitive
"She don't take nothing but DMT"
"It's raining glittering Radiation"
Opening Up Now ~
She has similar frequencies.
When you're in the Divine
You're in the Divine

Hard to Resist ~ More Resonance
That angel singing love songs by my side; Be Aware & happy.
A proper Sadhu Baba giving you the right dose of DMT puja!
"She made things so complicated I wouldn't even get a hard on!"
"God bless the Pistols"~ Flipout, Spiked with a Datura chillum!
Allergic to the dangerous Devil in disguise, dressed as a Priest!
There are Solar Enlightened beings ~ Shanti auras when you
look into their eyes ~ they're in the bliss all the time

Under the Pixie Flag
That chair says a lot ~ very dingly dell this garden.
"When I'm trashed I can find the camp"
Tripped through Tent city like a Gazelle.
'Come to see the secret Underworld'
In a magic, cosmic landscape ~
Giving it my undivided attention.
Jellyfish an Alien Spaceship.
"It's flyin' yu dragon"

Galactic Organic
The Betel nut for Mr. Flyin' smilin' Kaleidoscopic Pan.
He gets the nymphs. I think he did…full on Orgasmic entity.
He's of the Old Paradigm, let's take a ride to Jupiter.
On that shift with an Intoxicated Pagan worshipper.
Tossing all the elementals, juggling the stars in a Top hat.
"Our Universal birthright on Earth as it is in Heaven"
Thy Kingdom come.

One Cosmic Jelly
'In us the Awareness is the Formless ~ the attention to that
Formless in You. Lost in translation, Silence is the language ~
Everything is God ~ having Respect from Fear or just Respect?
Mass Psychosis, mass conditioning Id, mass media in Control.
Star Traveller, Star Travelling. Open to receive Universally.
Might not seem to make any sense but it makes people smile,
so there's something real in that, sharing in the resonance.
Don't make any comparisons it's all good, makes me happy.
Put her in a magical sleep. You're doin' it when you're doin' it.
Staying Centred ~ in love with it all ~ effortless awareness.
"I gave him a Pill, I don't normally carry the shop"
OK fine, "dosh out!" "A night in Devon a night in Heaven!"
"Met her as one of the surf girls and fell in head over heels."

'It's Not There!'

"Be STILL and know that I AM ~ God" "Who?" 'Divine Infinity.'
No beginning no end no boundaries, Formless it's not your Ego!
'Invented money, raised materialism for the ignorant to Idolise'
New World Order, Controlling all by Political, Economic Elites!
This Life is too Sacred. ~ "When you smile you do God's work"
'It is no sign of a healthy life being well adjusted to sick society.'
Dreamin' exactly what you want, It's all a BIG illusion, mirage.
Why do you think Fort Knox hasn't been audited since 1954?
Gold Plated supply, the Satanists turned it into Tungsten Bars.
He gave a presentation as a Real life but was only a Hologram.
Programming DNA to Love ~ "Then the hybrid guy walked in"

'Geisha Travels'

Pure of any kind of doubt.
Ride it as a healing ~ Synergetic.
Unlearning ALL Confusions.
It's the Teaching of becoming ~
Don't need to hold the Structure Up.
We fell together into a Crystal pool.
No more Separation ~ from the Cynicism.
You're in the right place and my name's Sunbeam.
Take her out on one of your special tours.

Repetition

"All the Karmic structures are no longer existing"
"What kind of Reality do you want to give yourself?"
Ascended Masters working through us ~ multi dimensionally.
Becoming our own Masters of non duality of non separateness.
This is Right, this is wrong, this is this, this is that ad infinitum.
Holding onto that 'Neti Neti' frequency for a Framework.
Watching all the reflections of your New Awareness.
You give this to Yourself ~ Your Freedom to Live It.

<u>This Father Was A Freudulent Priest</u>
"The duality is there to learn to discern" Not to be a Victim!
We will have to lose all our Identifications to go through.
You have to burn your*self out ~ to transmute in the heart.
Transcending ~ Alchemy in allowing to Love yourself
on many levels at the same time ~ in & out, up & down.
Doesn't mean you don't engage with the 3ʳᵈ dimension.
Show us the eternal in the drama. Going in the ONE ~
Put it out there ~ therefore it is. Nothing more to do.
As soon as you start planning you go out of the moment.
Lots of gifts to see ~ everything in harmony, a melody of life.
Enjoying each spontaneous moment ~ in the Oneness feeling.
It's the Pleasure of living it ~ without the strong attachments.
'One party at a time'

...... ::::<u>Mind Is Just The Mind</u>...... ....
A Big Ball of Energy going thru the Universe. "I'm fully committed!"
Sunbathing on the roof with a smell of burning plastic in the air!
For the Subject, awareness of the Object must seem to be insane,
delusional. We have to keep realizing this 'same same difference'
Panic to Hysterical ~ "I'll see you soon, if I don't get Pre-Nuked!"
It must be breeding in tribes living in Africa;
It's all, it's everywhere, the Primary essence ~
Integrated all the circuits in the Mind. Your Mind
and My Mind and their Minds and Invisible Minds.
It does sing ~ jumps! Are you ready for a Revelation?
That's how it is, that's the one where you believe a thought,
that thought that flips into ~ 'how it is' "I am into this bliss"
If you're to be here now everything is in Perfection.
"That's what we don't get told man!"
"I don't think they know?" "Yes they do ~ they are
reflecting them selves in their own Sun, Capt. Apollo."
Give 'em a direct Sunburst ~ with a Photon Tsunami.

Being a Slave

Is it an Hallucination, déjà-vu very dreamy? Trapped in your Mind!
Selling us the trick, that Heaven is somewhere else & Not in
front of you & Not in front of The Black Pope! Who is SATAN?
No one mentions them by name; Vatican Assassins for Jesus!?
We're all God, Heaven is right in front of your face now.
A Blessing in disguise ~ Life beating inside your heart

There's Millions of Universes ~ What am I waiting for?

Face just like a Bottichelli, Florentine goddess, Bless her;
He's a geezer. The dealings went down were a nightmare!
A personal power trip going on ~ gone past that major one.
No joy in that. So what are you doin' in your Mind field?
Psychedelic Ibiza, Goa where is that energy? Inside You!
As soon as the 'I' entered the dream started ~ I AM that
Characteristic of Mind, creating Maya. Unfolding Inside out.
One of their Drones crashed into their front living room!
I never know what I'm doing, as soon as you make a plan
you're in Conflict! You have to take it easy * So Stoked!
"It's only a paper Tiger but the lying Media makes it Real!"
There's the shift of the Consciousness of Life. All of a sudden
she was gone ~ chunnering at the tree. Finally lost the Plot!
You should be watchin' it ~ Siddhartha rowing a coracle gettin'
out of the way ~ on the river.

Good for your Health

At the dawn of the 20th century found a theory for Relativity ~
Loved Up not escalating it to Cosmic Disaster proportions!
"If I can do Theta healing anyone can do it" ~ Making life.
Switch on the light, doesn't matter under which flag.
Have to have right belief ~ Consciously
frequency gently quivering on her lips.
Goose pimples in the galactic Starship

It could go on forever
Serotonin * some people always have a Fixed grin ~
Sunset time with those long time Chillum heads!
"A long time ~ ten years stoned in the clouds"
She liked playing in the anarchist drum circle.
Not reacting you respond, detached, you step back & go WOW!
The last of the hippies living in a caravan by the natural Heath.
Voyagers forgot where/why they'd got their Spacesuits to live in;
Identifying more with their 3D body and not their Spiritual Soul.
Not every Guru's got a website.

Letting go of the Yin*Yang
Firing it Up with Full Intent, to be Co Creators.
That Frame ~ Sharing It in Crystalline Wisdom.
She had a lot of coquettish expression on her face.
Filled with free Love Spirit from everywhere.
You were a Goddess at that moment ~ smiling.
Shiva Shakti duality ~ Identical Identity
of your Cosmic soul coming back to you.
Cutting out all the different directions.
Having the allowance for it, coming
closer to you every day ~ delicious.

Want to be the Master
We're all Slaves to the five senses * inside my mind.
Sixth sense of Intuition ~ going with the natural flow.
Goswami experience ~ 'If it makes your heart sing'
Lookin' at each other ~ how wicked is this, don't bite it!
And they ARE so much in the GREED, such a big NEED!
So scared that they have so much money in their Bank!
So fearful that they don't recognize their Paranoia ~ If you
can't go to a concert without worrying about being stabbed,
what's the point? "It was fucking Lawless!"

My Dada Revolution
Meditative Hallucinatory faculties discovering Yellow Islands
Met Magritte in a tunnel; The Master of dreams having visions.
Imitating a call on a Lobster Telephone to Angels of Anarchy.
Explorations of Instinct and your body; Is there any Justice?
Unlocked the language of dance within psychedelic trance.
Drips & splatter, Cosmic colour ~ fields of mystery awareness.
Exhausted by HORRORS of Fascism, look at the world today!
Is there anyone interested in Truth?

Revolutionary Red Wave
The Power of the Collective through the Internet.
Living by the sea is Meditation ~ using a chemical Peace Crystal.
"Turn on, Tune in, drop out" ~ Shape of the pulsating heartbeat.
About as interesting as a Coconut to them!
Throw away the machine, keys and the lock!
Opening up the Zeitgeist ~
"No they're Not from Earth!"
"You gave me the kiss of life"

'The Little Pentagon'
Viewing a Model of the Peruvian Military Headquarters. Brutale!
Building was notorious for Torture, Murders & Disappearances.
Supported by the Fujimori Presidency; Where they living now?
Ask any Latin American despots or Global criminal dictatorship

God is a Label
Had a word with Oneself as you do. He Knows ~ Blob on!
You don't know until you go ~ Lots of Magic happening.
"There are those who have done it without cheating ~"
Use it don't abuse it. Here the Police know every robber!
They'll kill you so you don't make a complaint. One thing
being killed over Jerusalem another one for your flip flops!

No Feelings*No Sensations
"This is Babylon up the road but he likes it!"
Trained to Torture or Kill, Corrosive reality, going back
to life, regression and pulling up the traumas and disbeliefs
rotting in your sub conscious, directing you to another mess!
Here's the Perfect Heart ~ basking in the sunshine.
Gotta be right ~ isn't it!

Last Trance Saloon
Everyone just wants to fuck! Falling into heavy lust.
Head over heels in Love ~ "I like the windswept look"
'Happy hens make happy eggs which taste happy'
'Give Peace a Chance', Forgive your selfish self first!
"It has no value to me only to see someone else happy"
Jewels sparkling by the sea ~ Intense relaxation.
He is enchanted, it's a NEW day...It's a Pleasure.

Well Above The Law – Why?
Hyped up Government for the Banksters by the Banksters.
Government of Fraudsters by the Fraudsters & swindlers!
Federal Reserve never been Audited! Where's your balls?
They hold the Emergency Powers at the Secretary of Treasury.
We'll tell you what exactly you will do, where is the collateral
damage on the debt you owe us? Throw 'em all in the Coliseum.
We The People, got well and Truly Fucked, came back for more!
They were masquerading as part of the elected Government but..
Now we have an Imperial Cartel's Organised Economic Collapse.
$8.5 TRILLION has Disappeared; Recession no a F... Robbery!
Didn't know about the secret Prisons and arrests without Trial.
Then there's the Patriot Act's Provision for covert Abductions!
I can't believe my eyes, endorsing the crimes of Bush & cohorts
Ask yourself who owns the Global Franchise, financing it all!
Who are these International Predatory lenders? The Real Deal!

<u>'Protest Is Patriotic Probing'</u>
Oh by the way we been having a Secret Invasion of Cambodia!
Dropped uncountable tons of Dynamite on their melted heads.
Oh we did that in Laos too, in justifiable self defence of course!
By the way what did they ever do to you? In your Imagination!
Envision if you can, "The World Will Live As One", I'm trying!
But there's Political State Police on my street corner. Stopping,
searching; Paranoia rampant at the Top. Stand up & be Tough!
They'll Attack any Radical/Activist/Peacenik/Nice human being.
The Inquisition is all around in DNA, ether, Legal Criminal acts!
Used by the Governors to STOP Dissent. There's a long history.
*

Forces out there neutralizing all the opposition it can find, they
believe they've righteous moral Indignation, faith on their side.
Nothing like Conviction, let's give it to the UNDERGROUND.
'The only Solution to Pollution is conscious humane Revolution'
Deeply immoral wars ~ not surrendering to abuses of their Laws
Then what does the Statute of Liberty represent to you People?
Shine a light on Flower power, anti greed occupying Wall Street.
"Who Are Your Friends?"

<u>'A Threat to Society!'</u>
There are those at the Top causing all this war and disaster!
No Compromising on their Imperialism's National Security!
Arrested him, got ten years for having two marijuana joints?
Turning tide of Public opinion in his favour ~ "Set him Free"
"Thank you for that" Caught up in a horrible Political game.
Need their sacrifices! Need to keep Authority's Hate Prog. up!
Keep your mouth shut and just sing your songs, pay your Taxes!
Not for someone with an Intellectual force behind his argument.
Spotlight's on his Amazing Power Potential. 'What's goin' on?'
The Fuhrer's still alive in his bunker on the brink of non existence
'END THE WAR'

'Only Campaign Rhetoric'
What's he really done? Starting with the TRUTH…
Clones taking the troops out to war, broken all his promises!
Tell them you'll give them PEACE then blow them all to bits.
Transparency only a sleight of hand, deception to get Votes!
Made Pledges won the Election, told them idiots to Fuck Off!
Invested their Identity, belief & Faith in his cult of Personality.
What did they teach you at school? Learnt any Extermination?
How about FREEDOM OF THOUGHT, what are your rights?

Geopolitics on a Stick!
Takes Endurance throw in some charisma, Be Innovative
not the hoax's ~ Intellectual hand over of a mass movement.
Who is Promoting Liberty? Which Overlords are starting Wars,
engaging in Tortures, diabolical extra ordinary renditionings?
Madison Avenue writing the script for that, built a martial State
invading, looting state economies, not leaving a single rice grain.
Imposing a Regime of Carbon Taxes and Financial Coups d'etat.
Pretext of Humanitarian Aid whilst ripping off all the resources.
Demagoguery getting a population to Enslave Itself!

Toxico in Perpetuity
Derivatives are the Centre of the Crisis!
The Bank of the World is now in Control.
Pay Elites All your Taxes by Direct Debit!
You took the bait and now you're F…… ruined!
Pumped in money created a MEGA Debt bubble!
And they burst it; Need a Bail out or Martial Law?
Ask the secret Government ~ overpowered Congress.
Ask the Banking Syndicate if you can take a quick shit!
Is there an Agenda to control the Whole World?
Ask the Eugenicists, the Masters, of Life & death.
Classical Fascism; Cartel imploding the World Economy!

Aye Why Why ~ Paddington Green
Another Cultural Revolution!
Mao was worshipped as the Sun.
People as sun seeds turning to him.
An everyday object turned into a God!
Who wants to hold the Ultimate Power?
On Sunday arrested by the State Authorities.
Held for 61 days at an unknown location ~
without access to a lawyer; Not formally charged.
The World campaigned for his release and for ~
his right to creative Free Expression not Hypocrisy!
Still remains under Investigation, can't leave Beijing.
Welcome to our Anti terrorist Law, now enacted for 28 days.
The Government demanded it be 45 without habeas corpus!
Tony Blair tried to extend the limit to 90 days in Nov. 2005.
It's 'Indefinite detention' don't even need a Green card for
'Enemy Combatants' imprisoned by USA in Guantanamo Bay.
There's numerous countries providing for the deprivation of
liberty for indefinite periods of time. They threw away the keys.
These 'Legalised' Inquisitions are crimes against All our humanity!

Buckinghamshire Vastu Beauty
64 Emotions ~ 8 sentiments of Love for the audience's relish.
Equated to Nirvana, yogi in SUPRA meditation, left the building.
92 elements in whole expanding Universe ~ multi dimensionality
the dark energy is getting faster ~ "You either Live or you die"
They might be Spirit people ~ don't need any special muscles.
'Absence makes the heart grow stronger'? ~ ALL IN ONENESS.
Plugged in early at the Maharishi's ultra Consciousness Temple.
Breaking the Mind/control ~ experiencing the beauties of poetry.
Took you straight through all the veils ~ found it very spiritual.
None of it is important ~ it's only FORMLESS Consciousness.
"I drained the pipe and passed it"

'Thoughtless Awareness'
Working on the Sub conscious.
In between close your eyes ~
'If you love the land, the land will love you'
Forgot why they were really wearing the Space suit, that they are
Spiritual Souls not this spacesuit that became more your Reality!
"If you get enough people in a field tripping ~
everyone else takes off!" Anything's possible....

Be Rich in your giving.
"He lives in a Parallel Universe"
'Be Nice Or Leave' ~ 'multi jolliation'
'Time waits for no man, woman or child'
"The sweetness of doing nothing"
You can't dance at every Party!
"I'm a happy Dinosaur"

Child Custard
The Dealer supplying the Addiction to FEAR, Feeding Power
Big Test of Possessiveness, the lowest human trait, quality!
"Can't stay the night dad, mum said your house is haunted!"
All about balance, better health, well being, being in theta.
A sacred Mulberry Tree swaying in tune with the full Moon.
Understanding Love is here, we are morphing ~ right NOW

4th Chakra Galactic
'Huge high frequencies ~ waves coming across the Ocean.
Opening, Human hearts ~ Central Sun energy flooding Earth
monitors through the emotions and thoughts of those affected.
'Crystalline city of light within the etheric of Machu Picchu.'
With your own vibration, what do you wanna be, tune in with?
Your self don't pick up on their anger; No Copyright, no suite
of Slaves, sharing freely. Realise their light effects your light.

Bene*Volent Stratosphere

Orbital Friends in High places living close to our Blue Planet.
Hairiest stuff, what amazing treasures left Baghdad's museum?
The Secret American Government ~ Those telling you to Fire,
push a lever, press a button, pull a trigger, bow down & Pray!
Sittin in the desert watching a nuclear Mushroom cloud unfurl.
The Majestik 12, another 'Conspiracy theory' becoming true!
WHO why was Black Africa injected for polio with Aids vaccine?
Completely understand now why this World is being destroyed.
It makes sense!!!!!!!!!!!!!!!!!! To someone.

Wikid leaks ~ What are their names?

Distractions, delusions all leading you down the wrong way.
TO A DEAD END. Many UFO crashes ~ had human Pilots!
Many of them are shimmering Holograms for the distractions
of your heart and Mind; Engaged in the Illusion of the 'FORM'
'Won the Nobel Peace Prize for launching the most Tomahawks'
Congratulations! Truth is not always a pleasant thing they say.
Manifested, traveling across distant galaxies to open Stargates.
Chaos right in front of you ~ dancing with shadows on the bus.
Yes who massaged this Financial Crash? Who got the dough?
Who owns the Debt? Baron Rothschild et al it's that simple now.
Oops sorry the $ has died, had its death, so has the £ € & Yen!
Why construct a full duality ~ Isn't it a Cosmic Kaleidoscope?
Communicating energy in Pure thought ~ receiving Telepathy.
Primitives tuning into the big Mother ship seeing saffron Orbs.
Dropped out of sight, 200 million energy fields bending space.
However you like it.

Hippy dell

No Flags, It's all in the heart.
We are an endangered tribe.
She's a diamond of a nymph

29

Action Painting

Motion of flux, you ~ speeding dynamism for Total change.
Gazing into New heavens watching magnetic needles spinning.
'Not Art of imitation but conception ~ different sign languages.
Cubism's colors, ask the Futurist Manifesta sipping her espresso.
'Self expression & Deep feeling' having some inner Love energy.
It's all bollocks get out the way of all the distractions. #1 Bold.
The journey of self discovery ~ He got off the boat!
To observe your mind surfing ~ in no Mind Form.
In the tube ~ 'ALOHA with a sweet emotional body'
'Just do it as it Feels' ~ "Does it make your Heart sing?"
Otherwise it's not for you

Allowance is the ticket

"We're fucked from the day we're born ~ in the Matrix.
Sexuality & Spirituality ~ drinking mates at the Tantric Bar.
No place in the dream ~ lots of little Temples.
"I am the dreamer you are the dream"
The Love energy is circling
Be in the natural frequence.
Being happy for no reason.
"You're entering another Heaven!"

The Coastline

She's a lot of FUN even if you break your neck ~
You can have FUN while falling down the stairs.
"Land ahoy, let's explore; Found lots of free Coconuts!"
Everyone wants the Golden Alchemic, your beingness in the Sun.
You can give everyone the Opportunity to live ~ being in Liberty.
or be Governed, controlled, dictated to; Lost all Common Sense!
Lost the Natural Sense that everything is given ~ Being blessed.
Now you can see how they're making their 'Monkey Business!'
Losing Your Self ~ lost their Centre. Have you got the Illusion?

It ain't one of ours!
Astronauts Explicitly not allowed to make contact with UFO's
It's in their contract! Huge spaceships * flying around the Sun.
So much traffic they blank it out not a twinkling star in the sky!
NSA. is their contact with ET's * What was that orange orb?
"And that's your reward for destroying the Planet?"

The Cabal has a tight grip!
The Andromeda Foundation fighting it out by the Moons of Titan
The Death Ray "with this Plasma I can cut the World in half!"
They knew damn well that the Earth wasn't flat and its orbit
was around the Sun with all our other heavenly bodies.
Who's harvesting babies' energy putting it into hybrid batteries?
'Malevolent Aliens, Reptilians & Greys were not given a Star ~
gate at the other end of the Universe and so can't come back!'
We're not at the top of the food chain!
We kicked their arse into outer space!

'Skunky Monkey'
'The Mad Minute!' ~ Stress and strain acting on my brain!
The wrong empathy for life, does that make you a Fanatic?
Take a trip to the Lily lake in Kashmir and ask the question.
'Truth is the first casualty of Politics' 'Death or Freedom?'
"I don't smoke to get stoned I smoke to get high"
"As High as ~ Absolutely"
Never been presented like that before ~ It's in its Expression.
"I don't shop, I look, I feel"
With the music didn't watch the matter ~ I'm here for real.
Met conspiracy Tom at the Grab Bar. "Is it all Illusion?"
How you really Living it, 'The Proof of the Pudding ~
is in the eating', in allowing the experience to become;
If you put it in there ~'Consciously'- the Keyword to
Opening the door.

I'm tellin' me…..!
I believe that, I want to become that.
Just learn ~ to get outer the way, get into that flow.
They're keepin' us too fuckin' busy all the time.
So we have no time for Self. They teach us what, I don't know!
Then the Universe came around, jumped through my Star gate.
Somewhere it resonates because it's in the light.
Sending back all the right ~ vibrations.
By feeding it LOVE it will expand.
Which way do you want to create it mate?
Because you are Creating It! ~ Mr. & Mrs. Creation.
"BE THAT LOVE THAT WE ARE CREATED TO BE"

No Chaos
Nature & God are Synonyms ~
The whole Universe is in equilibrium.
Losing yourself in the Imprints ~
her feeling body and being betrayed
out of Love.

Unplugging that One
How each breaks the light ~ All uniquely perceive.
Transmuting the frequencies to give & to receive.
Can you hold it ~ or you won't get it!
You are It, the Recognition, trusting yourself.
"Love is all around, love is what you are"
You are made out of Love with everything else.
Just another Chakra, melting in with it.
Transcend it or crack up baby.
A good Love ~ helping each other.
They got that smile Inside.
Touching me with her rich generosity & Oneness ~
*It gives them Power, it's in the seeing*being of it, Live.*

4 Global Indexes

Freedom, getting up & not knowing what the day will bring next.
'147 interconnected transnational corporations running this World'
Top 49 are banks & financial institutions none initial producers.
Who are the international Predatory lenders keeping us in debt?
"Not enough Gold to go around" Controlling whom by threats?
Why not try using a bunch of Tulips like the good old days?
Or sacks of 'Manillas', copper rings like the bad old days!
10 whip lashes by law for any woman who drives a car.
As a Focusing Lesson, say no more.

A Pair of Temples

He raped & killed a schoolgirl on her way to school on her bike.
Who committed that Act of Genocide, Financial War, is it You?
Shot him right through the head, sliced her skull in half! Split!
Surviving on Normandy beaches then blown to bits in a Hedge!
We're not talkin' about Tulips! It's a Fascist Children's army!
Wrong time wrong place ~ a lot of Horrendous War going on!
Fuelling Violence, horror, Gore, turning it into Entertainment!
A heavy stream of monstrous casualties. Whose child were you?
Tiger Tank shot a white hot shell through his skin, bled to death!
Screaming his head off amongst the Carnage and Devastation.
Ignited everything Inside!

Livin' In Beauty

'To mingle is my jingle' ~ that's good. Rock On….
"Hey you got my mates poppin' when they don't Pop!"
"You're a Fuck Nut!" 'You gotta be in the know to know'
Bring me that Sagittarian firefly ~ she turned your head!
'The truth' ~ "let them think that if it keeps them happy!"
Saw a Dolphin flip, Kangaroos as far as the eye could see.
For Inspiration and beauty livin' by a psychedelic coral sea.
On a soft, pure crystalline ~ white powder beach, fabulously.

When yu feelin' it yu feelin' it.
In a bath of bliss with scented bubbles,
little orbs kissing you, head to toe ~
Stick it in yu ear and light it up!
Throw the picture, let them go.
Open the space ~ for it to happen.
Dreams are back, saw some fantastic
wildlife just outside the prison door.
On a different wing ~ of the Asylum!

Shakti Burger
Crumbling Identities ~ Enjoy the moment.
Quantum on the melting hologramic deck.
Transporter Room ~ Pixels onto the Moon.
Losing Time ~ Space, Spontaneous healing.
"For sure it's the beauty of your experience ~"
Your shadow is your best teacher, my Psychedelic friend.
Helping you detach ~ from the Mind; Watch the Oneness.
Take it in your soul ~ and let it run through you, all the way.
New Crystals taking over an ancient electro magnetic paradigm.
Allowing yourself to be eternal ~ no hindrances
Nothingness ~ coming into the Oneness.

Honey Pie
Bathing in female energy ~ transmuting, Opening Up
like a Pumpkin! You can break out of it.
Being ~ Nothing more, nothing less.
No duality ~ Equally, respected for her choices.
"I think therefore I AM"~ All Imagination!
Your Inspiration ~ go out of Illusion.
Nothing real ~ setting the energies free.
"Playing in the bath with smiley plastic ducks"
Learning to Trust Again ~ "We Are All In One"

'Dedicated Feast or Famine!'

Psycho War Ops, schizophrenic Insanity coming out of a sunrise
You can hear the Bomb dropping ~ smell phosphor melting skin!
They turn them into Killing Machines. They'll teach them how to
Kill people first then you can make your cakes. Who wants that?
B52s Carpet bombed Hanoi, what happens to those on the land?
'Never occurred to me that I could be the subject of a betrayal'
Article 8 of the Human Rights Act, see what that might mean!
British banks got 400% more deposits than the Government!
More "FINANCIAL WEAPONS OF MASS DESTRUCTION"
Sending your children up chimneys. It's Gruesome yu Honor!
They love making those disaster movies for US; The Horror –
Channel, 24/7 sex perversion, extreme violence, sadist thrillers!
Big Brother, Voyeurism, Paranoia, Government Propagandas.
"We can live without religion and meditation but we cannot
survive without human affection" his Highness the Dalai Lama.
The Belly dancing orgy ~"Difficulties are made to be overcome"

Colonial Bogey

She used to go to school with a gas mask over the handle bars.
Blew up the President with a Bomb hidden in his green Turban.
Cut the throat of his innocent daughter in Honourable murder!
Nice to have a 6 year old virgin bride in the pipeline too mate!
He chopped her up in bits, left her in a flight bag in the garage.
Couldn't make this up could you? What's next in the Assembly?
What's come over you the last few days? Keeping us all at War!
He couldn't tell her, he was on a mission. "It looks grim to me!"
He's a gunner in the RAF. not much chance for him then is there?
No not when he's up in the sky sat over a machine gun. Inshallah!
"Those were the good old days" They were except for the War!
Which one was that? Can't go to the pictures without drama!
"Don't think we'll go out much in the Blackout."
Gonna end in Fuckin' Tragedy

35

Enchanted Words

Creating language, inspired to be a Poetess.
Timeless, seducing the eye, lifting the Spirit.
Solving the Mystery of the Mind ~ Marvellous.
Hallucinations, Imaginations, Visions, Crystal wands.
Asked an Unholy Pope for mercy, he said "Sempre Non"
Choice of his faith or his King; Judged to be a traitor!
Found his head Royally spiked on London bridge.
She's left with his remains from a Brutal regime.
Women taught how to cook and clean
and memorise the Church's teachings.
Welcome to Humanism from Italy ~
Inspired his children in the Classics.
To use their Minds and make it Fun.
First common woman to publish a book.
Took a lot of intelligence and courage ~
Free press, translating The Lord's Prayer.
Her fullest expression of a daughter's love.
Let's have a Cosmic Reformation. Amen!

Substance in your Head!

Mind Altering drugs MEANS Your Perception is Altering!
Are you ready for that change ~ opening which windows wide?
Rewiring your circuits, transmuting your codes, remixing DNA.
chemicals, creating thoughts, projections, parameters, karma.
You want excitement, the sensation, the Holy Grail, Alchemy!
How will it affect your mood, health, heart, soul, inspiration?
Your being is capable of holding Conceptions of the Oceans,
the Planet, Universe, the Love of Life, a Sense of the Divine.
Where does your knowing and expectation originate darling?
Experimenting with a new model, accepting the intention to be
Self conscious, awareness for better or worse for ever & ever.
It's multi dimensional ~ infinite possibilities ~ All in Oneness.

'Feral Attack'

There's nothing more cowardly than blowing up a whole village
with invisible, unmanned deadly Drones Mrs. Secretary of State!
Shaking the Polonium -20 into your Litvinenko tea pot comrade!
Profligate Banks forever blackmailing our wastrel Government.
Fluore jellyfish & genetically modified cats glowing in the dark.
Development of Natural proteins preventing Aids in Macaques!
He got shot in Israel 'What was he doing?' Waving a white flag.

*

Mass Incarceration numbers quadrupled since the 80's in USA.
Private prison Incentive to keep the numbers up, Inmates mean $
Only answering to their Shareholders; How's your derivatives?
How are your detainees being looked after in their padded cells?
Lobbying for heavy handed sentencing, more Corp's Capitalism.
Promoting their business model, top two Conglomerates' profits up!
'The secret in their eyes'

All the Mod Cons!

String Theory ~ 'We met in Space'
You can fall in it anytime ~ in the now.
She went for a walk in the blissfulness ~
while I rested under a fragrant Frangipani tree.
Fanning her & amazing her with the Meaning of Life.
Finally she fell in Love ~ lost in the Maya of it all.
Forget for a moment and you're back in rebirth!
Fell into the Cosmic pool of light * heartedness.
You're in space right now ~ the Planet's spinning in space.
How many times will you trip around the Sun? Do as you want.
If you want you can go completely out of Mind's object gravity.
You're not from any Planet not from the material universe itself
Here to be as light as a feather ~ not caught up in the Machine.
Just being aware of the effect of it ~ all life is a Cosmic journey.
'You Are the Energetic Alien'

<u>Means: 'Rule by Thieves'</u>
Found Tornadoes swirling along equatorial Trade winds!
'The First Lady' what the hell is that title in a Democracy!?
Did I say a Monarchy, Republic, Plutocracy or Kleptocrazy?
Government of rampant greed, corruption, subject to no control,
fraud and embezzlement, the misappropriation of Public funds
at the expense of the wider population, extending power to Elite.'
"I Want Jam mam put that next to a tutti frutti, banana bullshit"
"I wanna be a Rebel being by your side"
Checking out <u>www.transparency.org</u>

<u>The Last Thatch</u>
'The Sociopathic King in his Castle Tower'
Travelers protesting to the High court.
Living on a scrapheap in the green belt
without the right planning permission.
Waiting for the Bailiffs.
Bulldozers at Dawn!

<u>40,000 Stars Falling Slow</u>
"I knew I would be safe to let you go ~"
Pulling us through the 5th Dimensional.
Riding frequency of less delusional density
Getting more into our own feelings ~
Thought patterns of conditioning, let it go.
Into Synchronicity with a girl from New York City!
She was in a jungle in Iceland, she brought me Psyche ~
delical Reindeer and if you can find an unexpected Shaman.
"I was on the way to Bubbles" The Star gate is always Open ~
"Need the quality of energy to play Chopin"
Responding to the love from Up.
Taking in the Cosmic energy.
On the last naked caravan.

A Lady with a Musical Hat
And the man who mistook his wife for a suitcase on wheels!
Awakening Mind's eye; The Consciousness Space ~ Traveller
A Muse sat beside Nevado Mismi on a voyage to the Ticuna tribe
then working at a Home for Incurables in the Peruvian Andes.
Fields of Identities, conditionings, value judgments, dualities,
fears, reasoning's, expectations, dreams, selfishness, illusions,
delusions, mirages, desires, bio chemicals, nature of the beast!
Less bang for a buck! Accept yourself for who you are, Lovely.
"Sperm swimming in her eyes" ~ Reflections in her crystal tides.
Bi Polar ADHD hormones jumping upstream with the Class A's
What do you believe in?

'Your Murdering Terrorists - Our Righteous Rebels'
Waking up the Human Sidewinder ~ Psychopathic Wipe Out!
Horrific Traumas of very Unsmart Weapons in a demon's hand
The Statistical Inevitability of Civilian deaths; Pure Inhumanity.
When you got money you got access. All Tooled up as an Emperor!
Scenes that some of our viewers may find disturbing but we show
them every day so you really should be used to them by now!
Violence & Executions by your Despots; Our deniable Tyrants!
Babylon engagement with the dimension, taking out the target!
The Universe wastes nothing ~ it doesn't die
but transforms ~ even a little virus like you!
"Who is the Alien?"

'C L A S S I F I E D'
Higher Intelligence ~ what are your Secret Intentions?
Disabled all our Violent Weapons! We won't change!
Armed missiles up their sleeves ~ Crash landed in Iran.
Can't even realize that we're destroying ourselves now.
Walk-Ins who came to save the Earth from Destruction.
Found 'Balance of Mind disturbed' ~ "You're Beaten"

An Acid Wig

Now if I can't find it I might as well be
forced into a Living Skin.
"It's not a Rant it's a Rhyme"
'Hippy Holiday camp' ~ Sun glinting in your long hair.
MDMA ~ Sunshine in your face ~ makes it all fit into place.
"If you got the sun shining on your arse why go to the cold?"
"You know he's got a job & You got nothing better to do!"
"Goan live in an oxygen bubble ~ not in the Real World!"
He did a Magic Carpet ~ Orgasmic trip, 'Just Enjoy It'
If you don't live it you can't share it ~
If you don't love it you can't share it.
I understand and do your best for all,
that's all you can do, right?
"I suggest you do it before the World falls to bits!"

Trip to the Fluorescent Market

What yu doin takin' all the Psychedelic ones out of the box?
Charms, flashin' rings, bracelets ~ hangin' from every orifice.
High in the Rainbow dance Tipi ~ get up when you like.
'Love is like Ice Cream it comes in a lot of different flavours'
A Happy Tummy

'That we're all Gods'

Good Slogan for a despotic Labour Party!
My new advice, enjoy it as much as you can.
Great ~ 'Because We Care'
Put a Star by that one!
How about other creatures by your side?
Swimming on the Land ~ with long tails.
I don't want to think about it ~ Clarify with Mind.
'You don't have the attachment but you got ~
The Unconditional Love'

Bacon Sun
To stay in the moment ~ that's the Meditation
Looking after your baby ~ Is the Meditation.
No need to go to the Temple; Who's in charge?
Spontaneous creativity ~ holistic synergy, energy
Focusing on the wave, having a little chat with now.
Read the labels, what the fuck; Why they put sugar in my soup?
One cell talkin' to another cell... lifeless eggs full radio activity.
Cheap battery, No Love, our Mind is in our toe, in ourselves ~
Who knows ~ acts Consciously not all about a dream

Global Air Currents
What's he carrying on his head? "A Fridge!" Transcending
the Pain that's what Eastern Philosophy/Culture's all about ~
If the Mind moves first the Chi follows. Directing the Mind
to move chi ~ 'It can only be what it is'
"I got butterflies in my stomach"
The cigarettes & a cup of tea, only thing keeping her alive!
"Blown the safe!" Walked a mile for the Perfect croissant.
'Something that captured my Imagination' ~ Crystal Clear.
"Be the Change ~ you want to see in the World"
Permaculture sending some lovely oak tree vibes.

Who did that to us?
There's no time to duck & dive ~ Part of the horror of WAR!
Somebody is Responsible for making this happen! In Ruins!
Carpet Bombing!!! Vacuuming up burning tiny bits of flesh.
Hoping you weren't going to be a Target; Trapped, ask Shiva.
Glowing bright red, girl with a pineapple grenade for a head.
Hiding in a lethal Haystack, melted to death in a summer field.
Where can we get some Protection? Dismiss it from your Mind.
This is the Front Line! Are you ready to burn?
"I'd rather be by a Frangipani tree in Hampi"

Promising to Liberate Ignorance
All the System's Rules, Regulations, Levels, Restrictions, Ideas,
Conditionings, codes, identities, illusions, delusions, Allusions,
Orders, manners, etiquettes, protocols, judgments, d/evaluations.
So try Observing from your true essential, inspirational being ~
That's who you really are ~ Lights of eternal Conscious * Flash!

Free Parties were Ended so was the Trust!
UK Gov sold their people out can't even have a solstice festival.
Old people's care homes, hospitals, pensions in utter despair!
Authority, Regulation by the Predators on your street and GM.
Cloned foods, polluted air, water, radioactive nuclear Powers!
Corruption of your leaders with their noses deep in the trough.
Dynamited Marine, coral reef, starvation is no surprise then!
"They won't start the war until we get there, will they sir?" Ego
"Who made the Gods to prey on the Fears of men?" SLAVERY!
Supporting a Maniacal Plutocracy instead of a true democracy.
Wise up! "The Slaves are Mine!" Cobras swallowing Pharaohs.
The Quest in solidarity with an Agent Provocateur of Inspiration

Playing the Pipes of Pan
"It is as it is, NOT as Your mind Imagined You wanted it to be"
So in other words, You can't be bothered to do anything then?
Ego disappointment ~ let's have some good Karma! Try Reiki!
You, Yes You can make people feel they are the most Amazing.
You've a natural ability to Inspire, shining your light on us all.
We're feeling your Stardust at the Centre of a Great Attraction.
Some see it as phony others get its Super Magical Creativity ~
It's up to them, what they're capable of Allowing ~ receiving
of this precious gift you're giving out for free ~ being Happy.
Connectivity high dynamic energy, charismatic force, E quality
of real beauty, great communicator, coquette, a sexy little ass.
Wild flower child * free spirit.

Equal Proportions
Pigeon shit, salt rock & Honey for a full on Aphrodisiac paste.
Misuse is Black Magic, try some Rajma, tantric hidden secrets.
You have to think about the woman's pleasure ~ She gives you
the Ultimate Pleasure back & what else do you want darling?
The sugar's been spirited with mantras, are you Infatuated yet?
You'll get arrested for posing as a Eunuch!
In the Palaces of Illusion.

Hari Krishna Explosion
His favourite sport was killing demons!
Thousands of Cupids below his golden feet ~
Each moment is Infatuated with luscious, sultry Lakshmi beauty
"I'll give you my Super Thunderbolt" Creation of Mystic Power.
Sex appeal of Mother Universe; Parvati she has wide Lotus eyes
Saturn's vision fell on him. All an Opportunity ~ Open Source!
Send a miracle with long red hair, extra voluptuous dimensions.
That's natural we want to fuck & feel & touch & love each other.

Juicy*Pattaya*Titania
Like a child in a sweet shop with a Gold card
being able to choose all the flavours on the shelf.
Put £10 in her fruit machine, every time gets to win.
"Here You are the Prize" You can pick Any one You want!
There's No competition for women, why would men fall out?
If you don't want it tonight have it tomorrow ~ "Up to you ~"
Long time ~ short time, she's there to Please You. Happy End!
Whores that never kiss, see a fuck as a bodily function not love.
"I don't want to put a woman on a lead, don't want a cute dog"
"It's up to you!" No really it's up to me but I'll let her think that.
Lao cow, Thai poulette, pink not battered! Lady boys for toys!
Just ask for the chicken farm, no anxiety for blondes anymore!
Ping Pong, body to body, unlocking languages of debauchery.

Fresh Breeze
with her succulent Passion fruit on top!
"2am and there's no cows on the road ~
you know life is changing in 'modern' India"
Goa ~ Tourist Attraction ~ Banyan tree in the evening.
First you have to have the right frequency ~ Aliveness.
Being with you, tuning in you, asking them to be in service.
Men in Rainbows, Angels at my command feeling our Power.
Losing the Will, being the Will because you are in the Will.
You have to put it out through you ~ it's happening anyway!

Kissing Lips
"It starts ~ with a Fuck!" then wants another!
Impossible to leave, living on special Space cakes.
Sitting on a Stone needing extra Poppers, Adrenalin & speed.
"Every love affair has to have despair" Whose theory is that?
If you don't come out of that you give yourself a f…g nightmare.
No more Mind pains ~ Sharing Cool love, quality of relationship.
Changing the frequencies of your own dis/ease Programming.
'Loving every woman and not loving every woman'
Creating the magic with the Inter acting elements.

Alchemic Illusion
'It's all fabrication of our Minds, this reality surrounding us.
A ground of bacteria on the edge to the other state.
Only Mushrooms can Travel across deep Space ~
Multi dimensional Daisies alive in a Tipi camp.
Just the vessel for what wants to be expressed.
Don't get in the way ~ it's already there.
"I gave her everything it brought her nothing"
In the 6 arms of Green Jade, Tantra Tara ~ Boddhisattva.
Bringing Liberation to all beings ~ through Cosmic fusion.
Contains but transcends all duality, look at les fleurs de Soleil.

'Intent is reality'
Alerted to Earth out of Control from the Nuclear explosions!
How do you know it's not a Helicopter disguised as a UFO?
Shape shifting behind the shimmering curtains.
It'll hit us directly on the Inside.
Clean up your hard drive Baby.
It's all relative, it's the Intent.
You go through the Gate or not.
It's singing to you.
'Spaceships over Fukushima'
Saving the Planet. "Thank you"

Fire Circle
See Zero ego let it go ~ through the Gate.
"No good feeling second best to Ketamine"
Consciousness Process in the Conscious.
Coming in the realization of our own selves.
Extraordinarily beautiful ~ The All In One.
One for all seeing the point and finding yourself.
Not in the electromagnetic old body of Mother Earth;
New in a crystalline grid transmitting super conductivity.
Make it happen more easy for everyone ~
Showing Yourself, holding the knot in the net.
"The jungle is the mother of all cities"
STOP! Be here now.

Like Alchemy
Giving it out and receiving it
Making it ~ Express through you.
Uplifting, purifying yourself.
Directly manifesting it for all the whole world.
As it is for you.

Poverty ~ Trappings!

So in denial of themselves, believes in all the Existential Fears!
To put themselves down allowing themselves to be oppressed.
They Love their Golden Jail with curtains & home furnishings!
He saw it in my Presence. I lived my truth ~ he couldn't let it go.
Sitting with the family of Light & Love, calming down anxieties.
Super Moons flying so close to Mother Earth.

Stoned Centaur

"Couldn't read the Combination lock!" need a Flash light!
Addiction, helpless as so dependent on the chemicals' habit!
There is no comparison everyone unique in an Individual state.
Hybrid Creation; Coded through the lifeline ~ to coming back.
'Only Adam, Eve and God know where The Garden of Eden is'
"I wish I'd taken Sensible things when I was in California"
Russian and Indian TV; Experts at spin and manipulating You.
Dumbing down people's vibrations to the lowest denominator.
Neutrinos clicking in, sharing high resonance of conjugal bliss
Finding rough & ready diamonds sparkling with less processing.

#2 to #6 Evaporation

Sex chakra ~ feeling body evolving to the 3rd eye...
Through this Insight you transmute your emotion.
'Matter ~ energy in motion'
Flowing over your heart & Understanding.
What do you want with it id? Your body fills you up ~
Receiving It, knowing who I am ~ It's only my howling Mind!
Difficult to live with your Ego density.
"If it's nice it's nice" ~ "If it's bad it's bad"
Ego is the Attachment; It's the Hardest part to let go, darling!
Let it be ~ You don't have to show you're there.
You are there ~ You are it ~ transmuting gravity.
Life goes on ~

Let her be Free ~ Let him be Free
What was ~ is infinite.
Don't want to jeopardize
that feeling of Oneness.
You know it because ~ You are it
don't need to prove it again ~
You got it.

Another F..... Curse!
God told them they were the Chosen people & they believed it!!
'Do you wanna feel my reptilian parts? His pert gecko arse'
"What's the best Commodity?" "Cash?" ~ "No black hash!"
There's a lot of Fakirs around, I'm not on drugs, just ¼ a day!
Sometimes a Golden chariot comes as a wheelchair in a mirror.
Understanding brain patterns to push visions through ~
There is an Infinity of Worlds, you build your own.
Appearing in different places at the same time ~
Allowance and being Conscious about it.

My Exquisite Muse
Sometimes just gotta swallow it, just not worth the aggravation.
Playing, cat & mouse with you brilliantly. She's Queen Mandy.
ADHD & full on MDMA; K line, alluring meow meow, THC.
Which bewitching path are you leading me down twinkling fairy?
Imaginary being ~ Shiva Valley Carnival, trancing cornucopia.
She's wide Open, "I'm having a great time ~ hope you are too!"
Wild spirit engulfing your heart in flames, burning, burning light!
Dosed me up again fucked up blinded by her dazzling brightness
You get to the top she lets you fall into her immediate distraction
She's free sky diving ~ you're drawing lines in a sexy whirlwind!
Full on floaty ~ "You don't wanna be dragged around by her!"
Makes you feel Supernatural ~ connection, gotta know yourself.
She's a gorgeous, pert invitee from the Lemon drop Tribe.

Peachy*Areoles
"I love a room full of confused women!"
No one can hold on anymore ~
We wanna let go ~ Right, Perfect.
Go Full speed ~ new approach.
Non compos mentis or not? Letting go ~ to Oblivion Nova!
Somehow we are there for holding the net too, into the corona.
So many Levels ~ we can choose Spirits from wherever we want.
No need to chase it, just giving it a FORM ~ for you to recognize.
"Hi I'm Debbie from Dallas!"
"All she had to do was dance"

Infinity Pools
Just living in a glorified, fashionable Trap ~
"WAKE Up!" Making a Conscious decision.
Processing ~ Defining exactly what you want.
The Picture is set, waiting for it all to Open ~
Fix it and be detached from her, irrational desires.
Describes Fully the Illusion ~ Active Meditation.
Stamping it in the earth, touching the sky.

"Drink beyond the bottle!"
Elixir of Male Potency ~ who got the washout?
*New Understanding of this Freedom * Mind Altered!*
"She's indigenous to the Himalayas, a tribal beauty"
Hiding from Intimacy need more boosting for Queen Mandy.
'You know it gives you that lurvin' feelin'
Living & Learning

A comic book of disasters!
Filtered the power of language.
A real woman is a woman
A puppet is a puppet.
Instantaneously

Divine * Doughnut at the Seraglio

"It's your legal right as a Man" "like where's that then mate?"
And the Devil, head of the Secret Police is running the country
Can have 4 women if you can feed them, who's on a diet then?
As much as your Ego can hold up, sign of status, honor; 'I AM!'
Reflection on the tribe in Global mirrors; "I Don't want a wife."
Sitting on the Bent Pyramid realizing we've lost the Live Sun"

'I've got the Kit!'

My ashram, psychedelic courtyard ~ streaming light in flora.
This is when you come in with who you are ~
"Be Careful this man is a wreck, a Yogi over doer"
Anyway it doesn't matter ~ swimming across a bridge.
You can get up here, looking into your self.
The sacred Messenger, go on ~ get Cracking!
You are a Big Rumi devotee

'Alone but not lonely'

Goa Full Distraction after distraction after distraction after ~
"never the last joint, don't Panic" Down to his last two drops..
It's all about the flow ~ you need an understanding voice,
some times when sat with yourself, Oneness, on your Enfield
or paddling a Kayak by an Orca in the straits of Juan de Fuca.
Thank God at least you Won, what would happen if you'd lost?
"I saw the best of you" High on life in that great relationship.
A new lease of living ~ She pulled me out of the quick sand.
Flip kick, pushing him to go ~ don't make yourself a slave.
"It's my life" 'Live & let live' ~ Young & fresh, Alive.
Experiencing Wonderful extremes in my dreams of you.
Not more doom and gloom; Don't want any of that!
Feel the Celebration of the Experience of life ~
Stop behaving nihilistic, you've gone all mystic.
"Who let you in!?"

Nature is boundless
'Humans want their cake and eat it and all the others too!'
All of it & leave a f…. mess! Coming here for their holiday,
entertainment, recreation. Others traveled here before for
Idealism & Higher Consciousness, gliding through delusions ~
Creations in my Mind, mirrors of Inside. Mitochondrial Aliens
don't belong to our DNA Profile at all! You do have a choice!
Project the Heart ~ Integration letting it flow freely, consciously.
Sometimes I let people drive me mad, are you a God
fearing man ~ how big is Your Memory stick?

Forgetful * Synchronicity
"Died in Samadhi full High on Opium cream,
one moment a breath, one instant no breath"
He could watch the Operation in their faces ~
A borderline to something else ~ flat lining death.
Only users lose drugs ~ "I put it in a Sacred Place"
Collecting -ve vibes, put in the Refuse bin ~ of the Mind.
Paying the girls to sit and play with themselves.
Count you in ~ coming to the Garden of Eden;
If letting it flow ~ full compassion of the heart.

What's the Problem?
They love each other but are not together…
How do you get to the Point where you drive over the Cliff
with your two estranged children ~ "It's what Killed daddy!"
Attachment to your own flesh & blood ~ A sad, loss lesson.
Conflict in frequency ~ on Overload!
Stress is the Judgment of the energy ~
The Never Ending Story ~ Nothing gets Lost.
It's the way Mr. Gemini ~ He's getting really wise.
Had a Venus line going through surrounded by all that beauty!
The Mind is the Universe ~ I'm goin' for an ecstatic space walk.

Sweet Infinity

Accepting the Cosmic as bigger than you can imagine ~
All made for you to Experience ~ The doors are OPEN.
Restructuring the Frame letting the other people see it.
Shuffle it out ~ with the Emissaries from Anjuna, Goa.
Making your Mind realize it, can't control Everything!
Giving them the Trust that it's all there and working.
Surrendering to magical, mystical Pleiadian mystery.
Asked us if OK to be a living channel
allowing them to work through you.
Followed my heart… FULL STOP!
We do it by being it ~ light hearted.

Yellow Seed & Red Snake

Flooding Yoginis ~ Fantasia opening the Space to Utopia.
Living in my House # 44, along Harmonic Hermit street.
Going for his own Truth ~ end of a cycle going into the next.
Everyone has to find their own 'Occult' pathway by them self
Dhamma energy is not to be feared ~ be it don't need to do it!
How do you use the Power in the present moment ~ essence.
There is Natural authority, the Cosmos, learning how to dance
through the Ego frame, through any Corruption on the Outside.
Natural Law no holding back, unfolding by ourselves the Lotus.
Putting the Input in to make the jump ~ through time & space!
Wisdom can't be Expressed ~ Wisdom is dematerialising of now.
Transmuting the manifested ~ Allowing it to be totally yourself
then you have Consciousness of it. Let go of all Banana bullshit!
A sound is an exposition in the Silence ~ building up into FORM;
Material illusion, you see through it, you see there is only Space.
How the people panic and they're here to show us the Solution!
Important to Communicate ~ "Look a daddy longlegs exploring!"
"I thought I was seeing things, seemed so unreal, surreal,
had to check my Geiger counter!" 'Click, click…!'

Tantric Poet
Now giving out the picture of Unconditional Love ~
YinOYang ~ what's in the middle that's the question?
In between is living yourself, free choice ~ Allowance.
Forget all the Existential Fears ~ be a Cosmic child.
"Every bird is happy why shouldn't You be happy?"
Your freedom transcends duality ~ first you ask for a Healing.
Coming together ~ Crystal Clear
It's for life…..

Simplicity is the Key
"Don't need the bus ~ take the quantum Spaceship"
Outrageous Experience! Over the edges of Oblivion.
'Contact' ~ we're all waking up at the same moment.
She wants to make it too good for all ~ A Sweet thought.
To discern, holding the line, intense and very smooth.
One day we will all join Siddhartha sitting by the river.
Understanding because it's all the ONENESS
"When I got my new born son in my hands I could feel his
heart beat. ~ Opened his eyes and had a direct connection
with our hearts.

"VIVA LA REVOLUCION"
Subconscious knows everything about you here and now ~
Omniscient, instantaneous time ~ space, It needs Expression!
FBI Alienating Youth, haunting us, finding his weakness tactic.
'You can change your head, taking the next step ~ into space'
while they're monitoring activities of the Subversive Target!
"I suppose I like it easy" ~ "Me too forget the Speed Kitchens!"
What do they want? "Letting me know they were coming for me"
Frightening moments, gotta have Mojo or Terminating your visa!
Show Trial, an Undesirable Alien, condemning him for his lyrics.
"We loved him for who he was"~ Everything is as it should be.
New Utopian, can you afford a good lawyer? Then you're OK.

Mango ~ Jungle Honey
Baba Libertino burnt all the maps to Mecca Bahia.
"I'm not going to Salvador with you Stone Wallah"
All those wet Brazilian she*male babes on the Playa!
"Take me to the local brothel"~ 'Female Resort'
It's your brain coming out; Being Outrageous!
Those little sharks & little snakes of fear on the loose ~
I have to lock myself in my room on the roof for Privacy.
So many near misses, don't look back, embrace her now!
They're still swinging up in the trees ~ throwing kisses.
"Grab my gun ~ Yeah, finally I get to kill someone!"

Flattering themselves
Tall & beautiful, curvaceous with swaying, long brunette hair.
"Amigo if she gets her Claws into you!" "Me I Love them All"
Why do you do it? I don't know, enjoying like children playing.
At a Lotus pool full of gorgeous women from Micro thong tribe.
Gettin' taken over by Alien DNA. injected by a bird of Paradise.
Offering her his best capsule of …….. Alluring Radiance.
*
She made it easy on herself havin' a clear Conscience, no blame.
You never tell them you Love 'em, what do I want to do that for?
Has a yacht in Ibiza, her father owned a successful sweatshop!
Resistances going on continuously ~ Super Paranoiac flames.
The New Energy ~ No Geographical boundary.
'It's TERROR all over!' Change to living Love.

Chain Reaction
'Reality TV' - Addictive but brain dead ~ try something new.
"Gangotri Pilgrimage, you pray all a way along ~ Terrified"
"Dear God Please let me live; Dear God Please let me live!"
You play mantras, magic, walking in the Valley of flowers.
"Om nama Shivaya, Om nama Shivaya ~ Bom Bolenath"

Freedom Is Inside!

Adverts did a good job on seducing women ~ to buy Jimi Choo
shoes, giving you your Identity! Visa Card #. Environ mental.
"I'm not looking for a woman to give me my sense of security"
Sure root to Madness; Now I recognize it ~ clear channeling.
Get on your knees at the top of the stairs put on your Sombrero.
"The Universe makes No mistakes" Consciousness is flowing ~
Unconditional cool love not boiling Passions of Homo Erectus!
Hormones jumping and flowering on pert lemon breasts ~
At least there's the joy of communicating, it's going on; It's Alive
Expressing Energy ~ Tantric sounds, screaming with pleasure
not that instinctive predatory streak in him.

Overflowing Flexi Sexual

The Tantric Temple is Unfolding, you're in the middle of it ~
"I don't know what is tantric sex; I love being in a cosy pussy"
Giving to others in devotion, part of a reciprocal, circular flow.
You can't construct anything ~ happening or Not happening.
At least get a taste for the journey ~ No Fear of Rejection!
"Hey love do you wanna come round for a fuck and a pizza?"
Living along le Cote de Bikini ~ to him it's a Beautiful thing.
Jailbait in your dreams on Tiger street. "Don't Condom Me!"

Hippy holidays gone

Not here for the ranting here for the raving!
When you see those eyes shining at you and a big smile
on her lips in a Golden string direct from Pleiades ville.
She embodies all apps. with the answer to everything.
'Why we're here today?' Soul creation ~
13 DNA strands falling in direct transmutation.
Swallowing a lot of lies, what is Knowledge
when everything you know is a lie?
"Very nice to meet you ~ Aloha"

Directions in India 11.11.11

18 turns to the left 2 to the right then ask someone... again!
He's building a school in Myanmar & feeding his wife & child!
You live in the bakery? Don't you Love it!
Shooting the breeze with me soul mates
"A WHOLE LOT OF NOTHING" Nice ~
Hang drum vibrating like a Spaceship.
"I'm visiting the Earth for a short time ~"
What are you feeling? It's going to happen.
It's all Planned, don't have to worry.

Cocktails of Allowance

If you're ever in a Native Indian Casino in the high desert
of northern Arizona, try a 'Blue Venom' from the Frog tribe!
"6 healers from the jungle arrived
they all put their hands on me at the same time ~
this Green Energy came in & I just got this healing"
"Then when I came back into my body ~ into existence!"
"Say it's another reality, you just made a Jump & came back"
"I want to give you Confirmation ~ of the Illusory delusion.
What's my Truth Experiencing?
Trying to find Yourself ~ going back to Astral roots.
Remembering who you are; Ask the Crystal twins.
Karma and Wisdom you are giving ~ 'Own It'
Consciously ~ Every soul is different.

Mind Games

Tantric Sundays, let's get naked, burn our bodies!
The jam of Love ~ keep 'em moist, very moisturous!
Living next door to a melting Nuclear Core!
Another little f.... blighter.
Get out of the pattern and let the Spirit ~
run through you

Super Moon Siren

'It's not about you' What about shooting stars in the night sky?
After sex she asks him ~ "And why are you seeing Doctor X?"
Found her bag of Cocaine, mistakenly she bought baby powder!
Such a waste of time, occupying your lovely head with Merde;
Prendre la tete! "Are you havin' FUN?"~ "I can only say Yes"
Doesn't care can't be with her! It's wrong you know it's Wrong.
Social occasion she broke both her arms and nose on Ketamine
Not ups & downs, an Agent of Chaos, Seductress to the Cosmos.
I'm here telling you the Truth; There is no Truth, it's how we go.
'There are Forces in Society who want to keep Mediocrity Up.'
Try a Multi*Dimensional approach with a Super butterfly comet!

Atlantis Pepper Pot

I'm a sucker too for scary, mad women!
"Going with it and hope for the Best of the Best."
"I'm reassured that there's nothing that needs to be known"
You go into the flow and give it a boost, intuitive coordination
You go for the pools of energy, where it's stuck & Release it.
No teachers, nothing to know, STOP Talkin' No Mind dictator!

Nice Little Yacht

"Anything True can't be Lost."
Sky portal to the Universe ~ Aligning waves of Photon light.
Our time for transmutation in a Solar storm.
Looking to the higher dimensions ~ recording my thoughts.

Cheerleaders at the Palace

'Why should we save you when you are murdering each other?'
Pol Pot's comin' ~ whacked 'em around the face, sweating!
Lived in the Brothel on the 3rd floor ~ down by the waterfall!
Seducing a Cambodian student lookin' to pay her school fees!
"You've blackened my heart!" THC traces in her Snickers.

Sympatico Glimpse

Trance Inside Form less Space ~ Existence out in Satori.
Decoding ~ Happy to find the Magic in Myself ~ empathy.
Same wavelength ~ coming together and expressing it.
'Turning on, tuning in, dropping out' ~ with discernment.
From what choices you give yourself ~ To be true to yourself.
That moment she has you by the balls! You're dependent on it.
All Illusions, your Mind saying not what you do but How to ~
Consciously ~ You have to go in the now
Don't be dependent on an Outside Object to satisfy Yourself!
'I AM ALIVE' ~ Realising what is a Body in the 3rd dimensional.
You take the Zeitgeist & write it down, you can be a doodler too.
Mind reflecting something new ~ connected to Source frequency.

Reflection In the Band

Even the chai wallahs saw the Spaceship!
Most shining when you are out of yourself.
Being Conscious about Consciousness.
Seeing you are in it ~ be in the moment
forget what anyone has to say about it.
It all happens instead Inside me ~
Finding how to be a reflection of Allowing
the drastic to come to Peace.
Experiencing Life and death ~
be in Integration.

Soapy Massage

Another whore from the village ~ has to pay the rent!
"Prostitution is an extension of Marriage." He said.
All about money.... Money well spent!
Get over this veneer of beauty ~
It's how you both might connect
Inside

Just a Big Game
'The Universal Blissful Pussy'*on psychedelic Vibrating.
Giggly, loopy anyway ~ Fully enhanced with MDMA!
Ecstatic Play ~ Let's have FUN, oblivious of oblivion!
Acceptance of the flow ~ that you are Observing now.
Just go into it ~ not the delusion, pain, the Arthritis!
That's a smiling T shirt ~ 'Enjoy it while you can!'

Oxygen * Nectar
"Look at your Self not at your pants"
"Suck it in!" ~ Catch your natural rhythm.
When you are connected the food is there.
"Felt no more place for input ~
'Growing your child like a God, rest are slaves'
Chaos and we make the Mandala around it!
Who isn't Brainwashed? Free from choices ~
otherwise you're playing the game ~ of duality.
Happiness is just a Concept in the Commercials.
What's the Potentiality of a Mind got to do with it?
If it's in there it can be Manifested ~ growing in theta's waves.
Why follow some shepherd, it's not You, it's not Original intent.
Catching your own dragon.

Exotic Psychedelic Toucan
Spent the monsoon watching the Peacocks dance ~
"Be a Clown!" In Goa the locals have seen it all before!
Everybody picks up on the good energy the freaks are making.
What's more natural than living naked on a sunny tropical ~
beach in peace with beautiful, hippy people as your neighbours?
They know it's about Happiness not the corruption by the Mafia.
Lots of us take it as a Spiritual act ~ more of the deeper loving.
Accepting of it ~ She melts into it, no thinking about the Future
just NOW

Manic Panic Park
Last defence of the Realm!
The Big Reptile in the Palace
Who Wants to be a Tzar?
"The only reason to put your head between
your knees so you can kiss your arse goodbye"
You do have a destiny ~ it's Inside you.

Burn it at Sea
"I use the drugs to entertain myself"
Promotion ~ E motion in motion.
This way it gives it a Special note ~
Gives it a direction out of what is already there.
Intention of my Highest Imagination ~
No high or low ~ same same Galactic brain.
Refining my memories' discernment of what I want now.
Not blasting this hyper negative ~ Alcohol, Coke, Ketamine.
"Can't walk down the street without having a line, meow meow"
It's killing the psychedelic, creative consciousness, sacred Tao.
Not just craziness, don't compare or put it in the fiery box.
You go through yourself by being ~ she's full Astral dynamite!
Putting you in a corner of Expectation ~ Knowing you're in it.
When you are in it you drop everything, even that you are in it.
Have to make Space for it to Unfold, giving it to you in yourself.
*Bio Molecular Eros surrendering to Love * feeling ~ her Cosmos*

Let the Idea flower
The seed has to die, working directly with the elements.
*This is the Alchemik * Magick ~ realisation in your heart.*
Giving it to the other not on yourself ~ Subliminally, sublime.
Letting it go beyond the boundary or it can't Unfold
as it's hanging on you ~ 5th Element of Space Potential.
Gave her a Multi Dimensional building Instrument.
Giving birth ~ the Ultimate act of Compassion.

Shiny Bauls
The singing Babas, bringing bliss to everyone ~
Always laughing and smiling going with the Melody.
'We all love to be in the womb' A lot of story telling.
"She's riding on the Crest ~ of a depression"
"Everyone is my family I don't have to be afraid"
Splitting up ~ "He wanted me for him not for me!"
The one who broke her heart; I know who you mean.
More acid brings out your Cosmicness ~ No Fear!!!
Free flow ~ of agony ~ always looking for the light.
"Nothing should stop it coming through ~
if it does it means it's not the right time for it"
"You didn't choose it ~ it chose you"
"My Guru said never count your money"
Choose the truth that suits your own reality.
"It's not a coincidence it's the Universe helping you out!"

Torture Nature
You have to go out of the body. "You fall in bliss" Unbelievably.
Surrendering to the PAIN, full emotional body over your Mind.
If you go out of it you have No Mind ~ left with essential stream.
Everything is One discovery from out of their cruel inhumanity.
Who could ever of envisioned that, hung him nailed to the floor!
You pray, while they're raping her with cattle prods! ASK HER
SCREAMS!

Consciousness ~ Tsunami!
Starting to listen, 27 Nuclear Power stations on little Islands!
Now ~ they've understood what they really need materially ~
gone from the richest to the poorest in an Instant, ALL GONE!
Clearing the streets of - Karma; Massacred a lot of Delphynes!
We're all wobbly splitting up ~ when the Chemistry's all gone.
Putting the Romance back into Trance*try some wet Sari Rock.

Master Mind Sin Drone
He sold 400 tonnes of the country's gold at base rate; Why?
Rumsfeld supplies Saddam Chemical & Biological Weapons.
'He's a bad guy needs to be replaced once We give him WMD'
Who owns the World's wealth? Ask the Illuminati & Oligarchs.
Be a Terrorist; Join the Stern gang! Now they're all Powerless!
Vigilantes on bullet street, Machiavelli Icon, their Role Model.
Solvent abuse "mucho gracias," paying another death squad!
George Michael jailed, smoking marijuana; 'A Public Danger'
Can you see any Irony in this, how about fascistiousness?

Little Saucers
Bringing Golden String Models from the Pleiades.
Came as honored guests to a Psychedelic Wedding.
"You've got to know it to Know it ~"
Compassion is the Highest love.
The Inner self is at its best.

At the Black Stone Moon Palace
Who starts this madness of War, are we Insane, so inhumane?
Try administering medicine at the Front line, become an angel.
What's the Intention, all this provocation to cause such terror!
Recognition, Awareness of YOUR OWN BOX of tricks.
In the moment is all in unity ~ Harmonic convergence.
The Spirits are already there mingling in the Rose garden.
On the frequency of Oneness ~ dimensions.
All in One * Synchronicity in the Crystal.

Gotta keep sprintin'
It's shifting, more Land less floe, melting Antarctican Lagoons.
'If it doesn't hurt it doesn't work' who said that? A Polar Bear?
How long you here for? Who knows, how long's a piece of Ice?
Conscious Allowance of the experience is probably the Key ~

People's Conversation
Is it called Hiking round Manali with my brother......?
He was our neighbour in the next room ~ Classic one liners!
Music direct channel to God ~ being in that flow.
Not being in that Mind
Living from our Heart
Not from the Head.
Perfectus

Invoking Oberon
She had a job she adored sucking off Caligula at a Roman orgy!
Patterns, designs, desire; What's comin' from your heart?
A lovely Program ~ It's not about talking Shopping lists.
It's what comes from your deep emotional centre.
"I've got a good imagination with Geishas ~
Wands evoking the Winds ~ Juicy light beams.
Sublime Goddess naked in a Toga sans paranoia.
Enjoying reality to the maximum of creation freely.
Sensualness, feeling the wood, natural healing stick.
We are healthy and well, if you believe it you are.
Just illusions carrying your disease ~ get rebelling.
Getting back the touch ~ having Life in its Expression.
"You're allowed to Love Yourself"
"Why don't you Love yourself?"
"I'm not...!" "Am I allowed to Love Myself?"
That's where it starts. That's the disease ask Osiris.
"If you love yourself ~ You can have that Toblerone!"
"You smoke? You, Yeah! Smoke in Full Meditation"
"Give up or shut up" ~"I enjoyed smokin'" Be True.
Your problem of thinking what smokin' will do, to you!
What would cavorting in Sodom and Gomorrah do too?
Being in the moment ~ not in any delusional Babylon!
A perfect Crystal fingertip.

That Burning Bush

Inspiration in your heart not Authority's 10 Commandments.
His tortured Mind ~ another Stranger in a very Strange Land!
"Love is not an art to us it is Life to us." Their Perfect maidens.
'Screams of Bondage ~ Freedom from the chains of men's Minds!'
"I can deal with all that violence ~
I've watched all the Bruce Lee movies!"
The Northern Soul of the Twisted Wheel.
A message from 'I am that I am'
*

Night Dive ~"They're just feeder not breeder fish!"
You were never afraid ~ the freedom to just play
deep down wondering in awe at three White tips.

Gob smacked

They offered to pay for the cleaning of their neighbor's garden.
Knock knock, who's there? 'It's a Wild life Sanctuary Fuck Off!'
I'm Regressing, Alzheimer's ~ "Bring it on!"
Young and Skanky not a Swanky Crackland head!
"I'm on Methadone & you don't know anything about drugs!"
I'd have to reply to her. "I'm a Psychedelic tripper"
"Mum I want my sweeties; Mum she's Ignoring me!"
"Take more Chemicals!" ~ Giving it your feeling.

"Please Don't!"

Your Worst Nightmare! It's been on my Mind for quite a while!
How can people, especially some men be so mercilessly cruel?
Where's the 'Honor' in violently Killing such a beautiful girl?
Where does it come from, this terrible Terror? Mad Catharsis!
His passion for his addiction, dreaming of your loved ones lost.
So sad melancholia, not taking the bull by its horns; Bring it on
with a broken heart, I know those tears, crying in the distance!
Why didn't you take me with you? Stop thinking ~ Love me now

Tantric Teddy
You have to die to be reborn ~
Put the old people and children together.
Granny & Granddad giving Unconditional Love!
'All artists are talkin' to themselves, Tragic, Romantic, Magic'
Different emotional frequencies ~ Mental disorders, chemical
imbalances; So she killed herself ~ dancing the energy out.
"If he's in it he can't be out of it".... 'Basic Principles'
The Secret Hidden Knowledge... 'We Are All One'
'All In One' not any distraction or distortion.

Incandescent Abstraction
No words to limit ~ the power of Intuition.
"Don't tell me that tripe ~ My Mind's busy"
You've done your bit for Society, paid your taxes!
"Made blankets for the troops, we wove the wool"
Had a couple of babies, followed the set Rules!
Now you're out of it!

Coloured Lanterns
Dhamma the purity ~ of heart.
Relaxing ~ the Mind of clearest energy ~
tasted everywhere by every one ~ moment.
Every time the Royal family build a new Palace they build
a monastery next door, Keepin' the Jesuits, high Priests happy
Nuns, monks and Viceroys on every street corner. How to be
Liberated from Unconscious actions when 'Ignorance is bliss?'
Drones & nameless Assassins operate in a Surveillance State?
Empty your complicated Mind of rational thoughts ~ Concepts.
Becoming one with each breath ~ one with each one another.
Becoming One Zen, effort & practice outside, inside. All in One
Entering into her little Temple of Heaven ~
Inseparable ineffable silence.

Absent friends
Our lives and wives ~
What a horrible Waste War is.
She lost her children in the dark days of the blitz!
Doesn't have any feelings left in a heart shattered to bits.
Immeasurable pain, sorrow, grief, Sadness, death, the LOSS!
Completely Numb
Love is such a Wonderful feeling holding you in my arms darling
Caressing your sweetest charms ~ so lucky to be alive with you.

The Love light
"You're an Artist, composing lovely music"
"I love you more than life itself ~
Everything will work out all right, don't you worry"
Passion running through your veins ~ "I hope so"

Split atoms virtual exhibition
Cosmic hormones' tango ~
'Bring It On' ...Love & Freedom.
New Alignment of the Blue Planet in our galaxy ~ Welcome.
Tingling in the head, let's get cracking! Stopping a moment &
realizing one day I will die, be dead, burnt, ashes, dust in air!

'The Kindness of Strangers'
"Tell her you Love her"
"You traded all this beauty for Smack!"
"She's HIV Positive and I still Love her"
"She's always been an original, my Alien ~"
So lovely yet she's had so much tragedy in her life ~
Met her on the bridge of sighs, she gave me beautiful flowers ~
composing gently her Love poetry, "A sweet, delicate Promise"
"Don't worry about my feelings at all!"
"Where is my heart?"

'Martyrs!'
Another suicide bomber at the Abdul Haq roundabout.
They brought their own helicopters in to finish the Taliban!
'God they must be really brainwashed them fellahs' Why?
'Men in black suits were just leaving the crime scene'
"We're in Controlccccccccccc Thanks be to God!"

'Complicity' (Gibson Enquiry/Abdel Hakim Belhadj)
British Intelligence MI6 Rendered him Extra ordinarily to the
Torture chambers of Colonel Gaddafi who was known to be a
Tyrant yet didn't stop them trading in crimes against humanity.
It doesn't matter how you spin it now the cat is out the bag and
your hands are covered in blood approved by a cabinet Minister.
Democratic propaganda exposed supporting their client Despots
His rescue pleas to stop the daily brutality fell on her death ears.
Give her a job in 'Team Libya'; Losing more hearts and Minds!
Methods considered so Brutal other countries call them Torture.
Our Enhanced Interrogation and Secret Interception techniques!
'Forsake the Devil and all his works'

"May we engage?"
Enough contradictions, lies, cover ups to ask is it Conspiracy?
Waving False Flags. Where are those unarmed Fighter Jets!
NORAD flew in the completely wrong direction;
All at sea. Do we have any communication!?
Where's the President when you need one!
Flying deliberately blind, lost in a massive systemic confusion.
A wicked nightmare for anyone living in the Towers of Babel!
What we gonna do now? Shutting down the entire country!
That's it, we're finished! "We're at War!" Keep on Preying!
Who's in Control? "Call my family tell them I love them!"
This is a Suicide Mission! Praying with a Bomb in his hand.
Authorised a Shootdown ~ Not expecting any Survivors!

UFO. of the Species

There is no Captain of the ship!
In the Purest of light
In the Purest of heart
If you're sitting in the bliss.
Feeling the bliss ~ that's what I think, not the word.
"After all that I forgot what I wanted to say" It's the World!
"I put the lifejacket on, got lost in blue with Jacques Cousteau.
The Total Trip ~ snorkeling in the now, right now in the know now.

Respect to All

He does a lovely bit of Latin!
"It's hard to see what's spin and what's real"
Intention, motivation ~ what's in their heart?
'Giving out compassion and lifting people up'
Experienced in Life ~ 'You Are Open'

'She's a Princess'

Burning other people's money 'Prostitution on an Industrial scale!'
The people you think you don't know, how can you ever know?
My skin doesn't fit. You're growing, growing growing growing.
"That's what I mean about feeling the resistance, all coming ~
we're all in the same movie, in that naked ceremony.

They don't tell us that over there

I love those Stoner's stories ~ You've become the Observer
Watching your reactions to the Old paradigm ~ disintegrating.
Can't catch a thought, confronting your own invisible fears.
Made you face 'Self' and what is in Itself ~ that sub conscious.
Breaking through the veil, dissolving the layers of boundaries.
Opening up hemispheres of your brain, whole Mind experience.
Think you're losing your sense to reality, self discovery journey.
Mr. Multi Dimensional ~ magic sacred geometry in the Cosmic

Holy Ponzi Constitution!
They're enjoying life as Natural primitives, no Economic Crisis.
No knowledge of a Global recession or Conglomerate deception.
It's how they live, they still got respect; We're not Tunin' into it.
All our wealth is funnelled to the top 1%, Imagine that and our
Democracy's really Government by Banksters for the Banksters!
All sorts of Fraud on the floor, a Wall Street Structure; Burn It!
Just living in a well developed propaganda matrix slave machine
Endemic Capitalist Corruption from the Very Highest positions!
How can anyone respect that? It's clearly the established Mafia!
The people given the Privilege to uphold the truth have Failed!
Met a Predatory Lender at my local bank, the High Risk Casino!
Playing roulette with your Savings and Pensions, no Regulations
Wake Up and See them for what they are!

Feeling You Inside Me
"I'm sure you'll be over the Moon with that one sweetheart"
Keep on truckin' ~ stoked by the river. Absolutely fabulous.
Worth doin' everythin' ~ on the bounce and get out of town.
She knows his qualities ~ Top man!
She said it from the heart ~ Full Respect.
Standin' me ground ~ for knowing what I know.
Another Sagittarius metamorphosing into a firefly.
"That's the drugs ~ Keeps you Open, to what?"
How does a young Indian girl have such a big Coke habit?
You're all together doesn't matter where you come from.
If he wishes to do that he's free to do that.

"She Inherited Two Bordellos"
"These Island girls are Really forward!"
"I went to look at a 14 bedroom brothel in Kuta.
All tooled out with girls ~
On a 1 year lease"

Petrified Children
Yanking your chain! You're Re/Possessed!
They love to hate him and she likes grass.
Quality of Life ~ the improvisation of fire.
Can't be easy pulling the trigger on a Tiger!
"Entitled to kill to protect my possessions"
"Take this we've been Bombed out!"
How about that for transcending reality?
Another psychopath enjoying inflicting pain.

Smack, Crack & Poppy!
Diaphanous Beauty down at mill.
'A marriage made in Heaven'
You were on rations while they lived in a Palace
Still the same today. What yu gonna do 'bout it?
Do you remember? "Give us a shillin' Mr."
Is this a Finance War of our political elites?
13 Israelis dead and 1400 Palestinians expired!
61 school children killed in their playground ~!
Who is ever going to make a Peace feeling here?
Knesset won't even release their radio frequencies!
Big Investors are making all the decisions and money.
The new settlers even burnt the villagers' Olive groves.

'DMT * Spirit Molecule'
Deeper into her pink kaleidoscopic atomic matrix.
Organic, orgasmic forms ~ energetic transformations.
Dodging the drips ~ "It's my house, Fuck Off!"
For finding women, go where the last War was!
No Competition! You're everything, All of it!
Overwhelming Love ~ going back to the womb.
Feeling you in heaven, unfolding in your thighs.
No structure in Inspiration.

Great Special Great
Coming down from a night far out with Mandy.
'Comfortably numb' the Mind got out the way.
I got out the way ~ lettin' it stream.
Absolutely in the flow ~ Definitely in the flow.
"Then I saw the surfin' video"
Right on Top of the wave ~
taking you Up Up Up ~ Go go go
dancing such a vibration, met so many people coming for it.
What are we taking the drugs for? Being on top of the wheel ~

Healing Universal Orgasm
They want to land on you & nurture you.
So soft, it's like snowing Orbs.
Peace & bliss if you can let it go ~
Feeling the auras with the eyes
In a different way. Feeling it with
Love, Light & Compassion.

Acid*Mandy
Being healed through worshipping, having the faith in
nature's way. The Art of oral stimulation of the penis!
Woman playing with her sculptured, painted nails.
'They left me with the spoilt dogs to look after
then I got incorporated into the Pimp's Harem'
'Dine in our Garden ~ beside the railway tracks.'
Prerequisite for a Spiritual Temple ~ a beauty spot.
They called it bliss, raving their socks off!
"For her the drugs aren't working anymore,
she's a pretty, paranoid juicehead!"
"I met her on the island ~ Bang Tidy"
Whatever anybody wants to make of it.
"I'm standing on your tail"

"Just happy to be alive!"
We live here! He made my skin crawl.
I woke up and he was sweeping my room!
What are you doin' here? Get Out ~ you 'orrible essence!
Tagine on the fire, letting it build up steam ~ to cook the food.
Alchemy ~ last instant synchronicity, Spontaneous, FREE man!
Spiritual don't do many Marathons got a Magic chemistry set.
Tapestry flyin' above the minarets, spires and smoking canopy.
They give it back magnanimously, generously, nice little bit ~
of Sensuality.

'Hovering ~ Officially Denied'
Light speed, advanced anti gravity, zero point energy propulsion.
Need a super fast shutter removing our optical limitation.
"You'll see UFO's dematerialize into the Ultra Violet"
Electronic/chem Vapour trails ~ Joints on a plane!
Alien spacecraft are still under observance.
Made them into Experts to spin us our myth.
"The threat never existed!" they said after...
"We haven't discovered what they are yet
as they move too fast for us to see." Ok!
Veiled from human sight just as Stealthy.
"I can't see a fucking thing!"

No Wife or House
Hair to her ankles, she is so beautiful.
Flexible, Open, No Conclusion of what is ~
Falling into something New, you didn't know.
To be Yourself ~ letting go of all the rest!
Getting your Trust back ~ Consciousness of being a live human.
You can't fall away ~ You are falling, embody it as a Co creator.
Follow your dreams ~ let your dreams become real, ARE true.
As a Bottichelli masterpiece completely Pleiadian, full of Venus.

71

'Everyone is potentially very wonderful'
Whole notion falling to bits ~"Have a wall but add some steps!"
Have the all seeing eye for breakfast! Incredible 'First Contact'
A nude Mermaid swimming with a supernatural sensitive desire.
So much traffic up there, above and below the Stratosphere.
Thanking friends who checked out Fukushima Power Station.
They can read us out telepathically, she's a Pleiadian contactee.
I looked up in the Big Dipper saw bright flashing lights at night.
What's a King Cobra doing sitting at the Centre court?
When you can see her Reptilian eyes and lots of tongue ~
In and out

Ascension ~ Island
Seeing herself going from the 3rd to 4th to 5th dimension.
Decision of where you want to be ~ doin' it for yourself.
Sharing our Cosmic expression ~ senses direct reflection.
'Coming from the Stars going back to the Stars'
Giving us the gift of Transmutation ~ fell out of our own ego
into a pool of Love and eating it!
Discernment we got in the 3rd dimension.
Giving this beauty to the Universe for everyone.
To be in their own frequence ~
You live it, you are it, you be it.
Experiencing our multi dimensionality each moment.
We are living in the Quantum Pool of Love in Love
We are Light ~ ultimately letting go of the Paradigm.
Whatever the challenge, letting it all fall out.
"You give it meaning by giving it meaning"
You allow it to Unfold ~
Change the Potential ~ to Alchemical frequency.
Finding the courage to bring it out from over the heart.
See yourself coming in that Freedom.

'The Best Dressed Sadhu'
The family of blood should be stronger than water.
We're through the gate and we're in the Whirlwind.
"I worked my Magic in the Portal ~
She was really dripping money.
We're in this Beauty together Honey.
Home is where you come to Relax & Say
'I'm Me' ~ Freedom to have a tantrum!
We have to do it for the kids.

By the Grace of...
Broken to bits, Your heart's not singing.
Wearing a Bomb belt ~ primed to go Off!
Freedom to make the right choice. Up to You!
Love, Unconditional Love ~ Not Terror rising.
That's the message they should all be preaching.
Not here to make a Judgment; Here to Express the bliss.
The joy of joys.
*

Havin' a go ~ just experiencing ~
Embrace it. "NO you can't do that!"
The Monkey Mind ~ getting' reeled in!
"It doesn't make sense unless you know
Something about fish" ~ Absolutely!

"What's the problem?"
Put him by the Bar where he was most happy, chilling out.
He's perspiring like a rapist in the heat ~ "I'll go sort it out!"
"I was tripping in the room!" left him with his gob wide open.
"You were right ~ I have forgotten the essential reason of life"
"The Universe is taking care of us" "Eat your heart out mate!"
Need to have a word with yourself ~ about Entrapment.
Then you've got Paradise.

Cyclical Command
Put out there by people and to be received ~
Our thoughts go out and come back ten fold!
Feeling it like a dousing rod; Say YES and get it.
Everyone will be blessed, that's my intent and that's it.
Just recognizing that Spirit ~ by a wonderful clairvoyant.
The Shamans all know it ~ had it beautifully demonstrated.
Balancing that thought changed the Power of the thought.
Don't give me tea or coffee just give me an Ayuhuascan brew.
*

If you want the Download on the Divine Heart of Love,
just have to receive the vibration ~ connect with Creator.
In the sky, in the energy, 'YES I AM' projected in the bubble.
"Stroking a Tiger's belly my heart was bouncing in my ears."
The Fins were up, sound of gnashing jaws in our psyches!
Into the dark shade of blue it must be Fear of the unknown.
Frequencies effecting different chakras; Sing me a mantra!

Being in the flow ~ letting go
"Looked after his schizophrenic sister, he gave me his tipi
while he went into Prison, took it back when he got out."
Hearing his Gaia songs, singing in my head with him all night,
making sounds, praying to purify me, expelling energetic toxins.
"It took me a long time to walk my talk" No self/Expectations!
The Shaman is inside me ~ I'm flying like an Eagle with him.
Cleansing ~ full of gratitude to the plant, to Mother EARTH.
Blissing out.

A different coloured light
She took her shoes off at the door.
Yin*yang Universal energy flowing head to feet.
Transmuting all the way to the furthest point.
Not disconnected ~ Conscious & Peace full.

Article 8 of the Human Rights Act

'The Right to Private & Family Life', ask any illegal detainee.
UK Banks been downgraded to 'Junk' Status! Surprise surprise!
Also a massive drop of Tens of thousands of beehives since 2007.
Are Diesel fumes stress factors leading 'em to a Tipping Point?
Not finding a way back to the hive when they leave to find food.
Contributing £135 million to UK economy; What a calculation!
Let's create psychedelic rainbows connecting all the butterflies.
Heaven or hell on Earth, people starving in front of the Stargate
Most of us are starving for love, Education, Acceptance & Food!
Job Seekers Allowance runs training camps for suicide bombers.
Fighting for a lost cause, No fuckin' end in sight...!

Anti vandal paint motive/Blame

All seeing eye, the sacred flower of life, sacred geometry mate.
Hanged the conspirators from meat hooks with piano wire, sent
their children to orphanages and worse, made their wives curse.
Agony!! Their motto, 'Order out of Chaos, Divide & Conquer'
Being In A Living Hell! Who dares to resist Evil and Win?
Prisoners of Conscience ~ Inhumanity in the Junta's detention!
Who's causing this barbarity; Who's having a smashing time?
"Let's go create another villain stereotype!" 'Savage Apaches'

Shakti Rockette!

For what do you want to Suffer; Is that gonna get you close to
GOD
or something? They fucked it up but we're just stupid puppets!
'He's the cause of all causes'~ Choosing which way to Paradise.
Goddess of Space all existence in her face ~ Supreme on her lips
Giving birth to everything that is ~
Lord Shiva is Time & he's got a Spacey wife.
Somehow it was noetic ~ subtlest of energies.
We brought them back into the laboratories!

'Doors of Perception'

Salisbury hippy ~ "Don't know a lot about Unlocking"
"Hoffman's micrograms and it will Open all your windows!"
"The freshest acid you ever took, Super Mikes, dots,
Purple Oms, Smiling Buddhas, Purple Shields.
Vivid paisley patterns in my eyes, not hallucinatin'
body rushin' ~ even if you can ride the waves.
The doh that sees everything, more in allowing.
Lot of unaware muppets, we called them India blahs.
Manali is loved ~ the Temple balls we were moochin"
A facilitator of the journey, you travel and heal yourself.

She's a devotee of Ma Kali

She was full hissin' ~ the blonde beast in a Hypnotised state!
Same Prana different package ~ devotion to the intrinsic Ocean.
When you look at God as separate to you they fuck up your head.
Religion tells us they are acting Directly on behalf of the Divine.
A Money collector with a Santa Claus mask & Police Uniform.
"He's part of me ~ I'm part of him" You're not the doer mate!
Nature's doing it through you; You witness it and experience it.
Doing any Miracle, like movin the Moon, the elements obey him.
It's the Mind, voices tellin' you that ~ "You are Chac Mool;" So!
Man's best friend or it can make you go Insane!
And what are you gonna do with all that Power?
Creating all that bad karma for that one asshole!

Lakshmi Pink

Khmer cooking ~ 'Happy special weed pizza'
Met her at the last sunset of the Millennium.
Spinning around a Star ~ the Sun peaking inside.
It's Maya making you believe you're an Astral Traveller.
'You Are A Star' ~ Already You Are Cosmically here!
Locked into imaginary dreams in your Identity of Form.

<u>Incoming!</u>
"You're in God's country wherever you go it goes with you"
Morphing, not expressing a body ~ mirror's reflection of light.
Who is taking any Responsibility? Who destroyed our Identity?
Now they're spying on their population, shredded all our rights!
This Dictatorial, Oligarchic, Plutocratic, Tyrannical, Fascism.
A New World Ordered Government, Kleptocratic Global Empire
consolidating, aggravating, accumulating All our Earth's wealth.
In the hands of a few & you got nothin' to say; Shut your mouth!
Wall Street's Money Monsters, Financial, Military, Industrial,
Complex taken over COMMAND; Stand still slave, "Attention!"
'Who is the Franchise owner of Global Conglomerates Baron?'
Fuckin' dangerous sociopath, megalomaniac, Neocons at it again.
Do what you're told or you will DIE with the rest of them there.
Chosen Puppets in face masks given the Powers to carry out the
orders of these Controllers in the shadows who made this Crisis!
Now they proffer the solution; "Can't let any crisis go to waste!"
Who saved the World? Give us all your cash, resources, to do it!
Secret Governments at your disposal, enslaving anyone you like.
'Gave a Facelift to Fascism'

<u>Predatory Banksters' Strategy</u>
Transferring all Wealth Off shore, sticks it in an Illuminati bank.
Who has Real Economic War Power, Cutting Credit & Liquidity?
Repeating the Slogans, Bilderberger's, Trilateral Commission's,
Council of Foreign Relations, throw in Jesuits too; Owning You!
No more criminal than that, Capitalist venture's looting systems!
Who Bankrupted the World, where did all the people's money go?
Scientifically Engineered - controlling all Global Market Forces.
Big Brother despotism down at your local Gladiatorial Coliseum.
Consolidating All Financial Energy under Maximum Sunspots.
Dow Jones took over Union Carbide, revoked all responsibility.
Ask what we gonna do, 200,000 babies being born every day!

Original Slogan > 'DECLARE PEACE'
He's a 'Peaceful Revolutionary'
And She's a Creative Genius…
"The World about me was going up in flames!"
"Don't want any fuckin' Peaceniks here!"
Who is "MAKING WAR NOT LOVE?"
Untouchable Dalits ~ "Not the time for Negative thoughts"
Identifying me as an Infidel or impure isn't that a racist!
"ALL WE ARE SAYING IS GIVE PEACE A CHANCE"
"Who can possibly be Opposed to that?" Really!
The Government was there to scare people into Fighting WARS!
Try Fighting for Peace, Happy Feelings, Generosity and Bliss.
Not the chanting of The Battle Hymn throw it in the rubbish bin.
Unless someone attacks you violently first, give 'em ~ wu-wei.
Try again & again Promoting World Peace & delightful Love.

"He's My God Tonight"
USA. land of the Free & the brave! Now home to 5% of World's
population but 25% of its Prisoners. 'Unpopular wars effecting
people, You!' Well Fuck Off! Possibility of Standing up to Power
'GIVE POWER TO THE PEOPLE'
Don't play the system's game, caught up reacting with Violence.
Beaten in Chicago's streets, putting flowers in Army rifle barrels!
"The Whole World Is Watching" "Say You Want A Revolution"
"Life Is too Sacred, Stop the War" ~ "Put an End to War, atrocity"
"GIVE PEACE ANOTHER CHANCE"~ What is your Priority?
Anthem of a New Anti War movement. What's happening today?
"WE SHALL OVERCOME"~ that's a good old Social tune too.
'WAR IS OVER, If You Want it' Who the fuck doesn't want that?
Grab it by the balls, don't let it slip through your fingers again!
It's cheaper than anyone's Life brother or another sister's Pain.
"MAKE LOVE NOT WAR ~ let's all live in Peace and Harmony."

Flying Trip
Chinese music carving Tigers and swirling roses in my Spirit.
You build with practice & self control, controlling your Mind!
You're feeling like an angel, everything you wanted came true.
When I got dusted, trying to play darts on PCP.
Smokin' hash for thousands of years.
Talkin' to his flip flops about K holes
Good acidic neural networks, cruising along route 66.
Ketamine just say 'Neigh' ..He was messy, she was stroppy
'AT LEAST BE HAPPY'
Learning as you go in & out ~ Charms of a poppy!
"Why would anyone NOT want to be Happy!?"
Said my philosophy teacher from Novo Benaras.
"If you got 'em don't waste them"

Psychedelic King
Comes out in the art ~ in the air, blessed, blessedness.
Sent an experimental photonic particle to the Vatican.
Be yourself Baba, that's all you gotta be, not so holy!
Careful opening the door; Everything as it should be.
It's only your mind playing tricks (on him/her or them)
Genetic belief systems, Mass conscious patterns/imprints.
"Health is a State of Mind ~ not stuff!"
Fresh British eggs from caged hens.

Pecking Duck!
You can do what you like! Regressed repression.
Don't Accept the FEAR, Recessionista! LAUGH!
Let's pray together ~ live drama. 'For Officers Only'
'Sacrificed the working class ~ flower of a Nation!'
First time she got a Telegram and it was terrible!
Fixed bayonets, over the top to your death!
Digesting the juices, the worry is eating you.

'Poetry is a dream'
"All good ideas arrive by chance" bit of Psychic Automatism
'What about Madness, Terror, Death on an Industrial Scale?'
Ask a passing Sperm Whale ask a Dadaist rejecting ALL war.
Let's try the 'Irrational' as the other side's destroyed the World!
Couldn't see a Kindred spirit for the collateral damage & blut.
Isn't that Psychoanalysis gone berserk? Surprise discovery ~
Intuitive*Surrealism.

Sub Juiced Biomorphic Verde.
Asked my Astrologer if I would meet a sexy Alchemista.
Needing some Energetic spontaneity ~ sweetly Cherie.
"Let's have some internal freedom without conformation
or violating what is true of natural reality ~ equanimity"
"No direct association with any visible experience but in
them one recognizes the principle and passion of Organisms"
Passing through the dark with Plasma balls of Irrationality.
I love the dreamy quality; Poetry of vision ~ lyricism, melody.

Firing Off
Your body's livin' off these toxins!
Are you givin' each other enemas?
They can't plug the leak anymore!
We are in your mind ~ I must be inside my brain.
Could see all these gigantic things connecting ~
Fear of Imminent death ~ I prefer its acceptance.
Injected with the venom, they call it dodgy inoculation.
The way the electrons are spinning round the nucleus.
'Science only interested in the Objective, Mediated by society'
Let's expand the Interactive human Mind, all being in it together
"Nothing to get we already are"
"He's from Brighton not a Zulu!"
Wake up ~ it's all you...

Into a deep feisty ornate fertile hard drive
New Alien Guidance; Why didn't you say, what do you want?
Pixieing on the land, buzzing around; You ever been happy?
Where's honour & respect & Love? Experiencing a few things
together, that neither of you know ~ many revealing moments.
They want to Open your body all the time. Don't put me there!
You're here to have your experience of your*self development;
Not conditionings of your mother; Hi Ho that's her experience.
We've each got our own movie runnin, how's your funny drama?
Learning together, fuck it off, have to Observe your whole self.
A belief is only a thought you keep thinking 'cause you believe it
Get it into your river of Peace ~ sparkling on Crystalline shores.
Comin' on ether ~ conscious time to let loose the creative juices.
You are what you think and can BECOME that in the stream.
Why didn't they tell me that when I was younger? Which ~
Matrix do you want? Magic, true alchemy, nobody said a word.
Now we're all focused on Peace, Love, Compassion, Equanimity.
Dancing in a land of harmonic convergence, pleased I am here.
More you live it like that less crazy ones come into your World.
Lost all Judgment, bollocks that someone could be dictating it.
A belief is only a thought you think so let's have that as a belief!
Healings on all kinds of Levels ~ You have choice.

In the Realisation
That's all you can wish for your friends, HEALTH.
You want something that's gonna make you HAPPY.
We do have a choice it doesn't have to be that way ~ Allowance.
Shamans talk it, have I heard it? I wish they'd told me sooner.
Self discovery is the best trip ever. How you allow yourself to
Open up to things. You feel and enjoy, to see, to experience it.
Get out of the way of yourself, let the energy flow through you.
"Cracked it on the head" ~ Forget the bullshit just be the love.
Crossing the Universe ~ faster than light.

To take the abuse or not!
Stay in the playful ~ don't take yourself too seriously.
We only come out for the Fun.
Off for a moment of Oneness.
I just grew up with that view.
No one knew what that was about ~
but they went into it with a good heart.
The energy was so good it blew me away.

Living on a beautiful vibe
She's free ~ just flowing
You know she knows and is in the flow of…
"Without ego there is no creation to ~
challenge the Mind or block the way!"
Only an egoist would say that.
It's all creation which is Perfect.
Their music changed the Planet.
Energy in the connect ~
energy of the times.

Energy Play
How the Observer is unfolding ~
In the indivi/duality of the Taoist way.
The truth path + - this or that, male, female.
In the middle of discernment ~ YinOYang.
You *Are *All.

New Year Mandala
Who has the Biggest Fireworks!?
Relax and fall into your death ~ breath.
Don't go in the Mind go in the feeling.
Fire element where we ~ transmute the Golden box.
Totally Feng Shui gives the Rainbow sensuality.
"An Indian freak ~ is a proper Baba!"

Ascension
Being in the One ~ Affirmation
No more the fractal of duality ~
We have to allow ourselves to ascend.
Fall in and drop our egos and go in One.
Electro magnetism is transmuted thru crystals.
1 ~ 2, Male female, O is the child ~ the Orgasm!
This is the feeling part ~ immersed being in the Ocean.
All One

A Gift of Rejection
Ego Maniac passion with the Biggest Tits & pussy.
A shift of Perception, it's all beautiful, no judging!
Only in the Opening of the moment ~ is it always
*in and can't fall out of the Magic * Pop Physics.*
Whole brain over the Allowance of the new DNA.
Quantum Illogical beyond the Mind's illusions ~ in the present.
Faster than speed of light, the 4th Chakra of Unconditional Love.
5th dimension playing with the elements of life ~ It's in the Stars.

Their Watchword
I like 'Bhakti Shakti' not Batty! Talkin' the good shit.
It's Yoga ~ Squirt the Honey, if you please!
I feel the bliss ~ when I'm warm with you but it's ALL Bliss.
EXPERIENCE WITH LOVE.
It's fuckin' simple, yet the Best kept secret!
Was sittin' on the beach in that Goa vibe, got nothing left to do.
It's hard to put a word to it, Mr. Observer, different lifestyle.
Realisation that you're actually feeling it ~ Cosmic air.
More Original, I like it ~ Can't stop the resonance.
Without saying it's this or this or this or this or that.
Live it, Breathing it becoming it ~ being it, all Prana.
Compassion, Unconditional Love ~ What a Great Life.

Miracles do happen.
Celebrating the moment ~
Enriching all our senses.
Smelling the Rose garden
feeling your touch ~ Tantra Mantra.
Embracing her energetic, wet lips.
Reconfirming their Cultural Ideal
~ not in a single parent family!

Flying Ecstasy Tea
Bombarded by black magic; You can see you are only Lurv!
Omnipresence ~ Melting in the bliss of Ecstasy.
Full Orgasmic what comes after that? Oneness.
Realise experience can be costly ~ getting out of the world.
Freedom allows you easier to make the changes ~
leading your mind into awareness of the matrix, of Om Shanti.
Don't talk to me of all the words of Slavery; I want to be FREE!
"Flesh and blood cannot enter the Kingdom of Heaven"
Until she's deprogrammed. Catch the mood, FEELING LIGHT

Lip Service
Are you sure it's the chanting?
Put him off eating ~ the Hologram.
We've all been duped. Paying a Price for…
Express your own relationship with creation.
Just criminal enterprise at the next Higher level.
"I jokingly asked Adolf about the little grey men"
Only the Operatives for the Masters of the Universe.
Let's have a HAPPY playground in Shanti Park!
Gorgeous ~ "I dare you to have that much Fun!"
"Wouldn't you wanna run the World Captain?
"No I'm too busy Enjoying Myself"
"SS. Eat your heart out!"

<u>Welcome to the Kasbah</u>
"Do you wanna be trained as a gland Piercist?"
Don't put me in there! 'The Operating Room'
Decorated her with deer dung in a world of Predators!
Very soon everything's gonna get twisted, just ride this one out.
Resonance and a Beat of a vivid psychedelic rainbows.
He's very fond of fungus ~ learning how to make wings.
Treasures on display * calling for a Celestial play mate.

<u>Damnation Bomb</u>
Who's got the biggest weapon, the deadliest gun?
Most Massive Fire Power sent us Napalm for breakfast!!
Who's capable of using them? Any Zombies out there?
How much do you love I Am?
"I couldn't exist without him!"
'KEEP CALM AND Don't FUCK EM OFF'
"Did you just spit at me ~ dear?"
Flood it with Light!

<u>Reality ~ under Palm trees</u>
Everyone is here for different things coming from the same ~
No beginning with no end; Gotta know yourself to be yourself.
It's set up not to be aux naturals but an unfathomable Matrix.
I have to lock myself in my room on the roof to get some Peace!
If you don't know which muscles to exercise, exercise them all.
Who organized that Dark Lord? Ask a gentle Druid or a Zeus.
I'm living on the beach beside the Indian Ocean with the wild
Tsunami of Life; I felt it ~ jumped through it and I've done it.
They're going down to nothing, can't stand to be in the bright!
Blowing all the circuits ~ Sent into Anarchy, Alchemy, Chaos.
Now you've come into the light, drop the Ego, drop the losses,
don't give a toss, got out the system, dropped out ~ a drop out.
When we left the Magic Bus

ALL THAT IT IS

Attracting my Soul mate, mate ~ You can have that feeling too.
Loosin' the juice, smacks you in the face! Nothing more egotist
than your Obsession with Your Liberation's own Enlightenment!

Connection - Life is a dance ~ If you left it be

We dance close, intuitively & sometimes far apart.
Just following your Mind, body to the heart.
It's lovely sitting ~ In the Sun ~ Worshipping.
Great Central Solar source ...which is everything.
Gives unconditional love, non judgment, life force.
It is the Abundance ~ is light is love.
The heart flame ~ of all that is ~ Unconditional Love.
Just gives and gives, gives and gives forever & forever.
Our inheritance to be in the joy, in the bliss.
I love it all, I love it all. Loving is an essential part of it all.
Love trance n dance ~ to stay in love with everything.
"I love you" ~ "I LOVE IT ALL" ~ Sacred Marriage.
We are the love, so be it ~
Evolution of love I believe it, they live it.
It's a needy love draining your cup
if you haven't the joy of joy.
Here to experience it, ready, it's staying in love with it all,
having that enhanced grounded harmony ~ free of gravity.

The Angel Frame

Solar Crystal net frequency over electro - magnetic grid.
A less dense vibrational field ~ Firing up the Diamond.
Made a Ceremony to Jupiter at Machu Picchu.
Overlapping the Tao in Zero Point Field.
Holding Up the Center of the Heart.
Dualities dancing the Lambada.
Giving it the Spirit

<u>One white magical butterfly</u>
All the coloured ones have disappeared just like that.
No one knows where and the bees, where they gone ~?
Need them for pollinating the flowers not toxic cabbages!
3 years without their honey and the humans will be extinct.

<u>Even Saudis don't eat pigeons!</u>
But do like to get married to baby girls rockin' in the cradle.
Girls attacked with acid on their way to school; Head teacher
murdered by the Taliban, reminds me same in U S' Guatemala.
"Is this Real World or an Exercise?" "It's not a f…. exercise!"
Cheney concluded it's Terror! Do you remember your 'Kaibiles?'

<u>'Under Riyadh' (Paraphrased, Wall Street Journal, 8/2011)</u>
A Senior Saudi Cleric has issued a religious ruling making it
'permissible for fathers to marry off their young daughters
even if they are in the cradle' "But it isn't permissible for
their husbands to have sex with them unless they are capable
of being placed beneath and bearing the weight of the men."
That Shariah religious ruling now called a Fatwa decreed by
Sheik al-Fawzan acting for prepubescent girls and Islamic men.
"Those who are calling for a minimum age for marriage should
fear God and not violate his laws or try to legislate things God
did not permit" Men can have up to four wives if they can be fed.
The King's suggestion that 'Women should now be allowed to
work as supermarket cashiers, only for the job to be ruled off
limits to the gender by the Grand Mufti, the country's highest
religious leader. Women can't work, drive or be allowed to
travel abroad or undergo surgery without the permission of
a male relative. The clergy have stood behind the Kingdom's
ruling family by issuing fatwas barring political protests while
the government appears to back off promoting social changes'
Where does Saudi Arabia stand in the modern family of nations?

87

Belief System

Completely twisted, I was living it! Testing your Pill at the door.
What a free spirit that was! On a sense of adventure ~ early on.
So they make sure everyone's having a good time; Thank you.
Enjoying It get out of the way, no resistance, less blockages ~
Breaking through, being in the creative mix ~ Spontaneous.
"but No way I want to be in the band ~ No Ego ~ Perfect"
Change the pattern of the thought ~ taking off the veil just to be.
Electric guitar full jamming, play it for the sound that comes out.
In streams of free consciousness.

Very Dreamy

Who took over control of all the Opium growing in Afghanistan?
Take me walkin' ~ show me things! 'When it happens it happens'
They're off their head, you're off your head; Being on the edge!
We're Trusting tribal, Trust to trust ~ letting it happen in Peace.
Twangled Hell's Angels. Be Silent ~ Count your Blessings!
I would if I could but I can't so I won't; Full of Resistance!
It translates because he's speaking the Truth ~
Death ~ Probably didn't expect it; "Surprise!"
Your spirit pops through when you left your body.
Breaking light coming out.

To Know

I come from Ibiza, nice people ~ Need at least this hippy vibe.
Never known a time when Artists were more free, Liberty to be;
Open & Creative opportunities to express true, deeper feelings.
Make it as Wonderful as you can; 'You're having a good time'
Lookin' at the old paradigm and letting it go, just movin' on ~
You do what you do and that's you. Goa's got something I like.
Flower Power ~ You're built before you come out ~ ejection!
The genes baked with Organic yeast. "I'm the sunshine story"
"I was really lucky with my Diamond Crown" Pure release!

Forked Tongues Dispelled from the Inter-net!
A Tyrannical Despot they'd supported for over 30 brutal years!
$1.3 billion/ year, a gift from the US to follow in their direction.
Not support for those claiming Democracy; Contradiction, irony
Last refuge of a bloody Maniac murders his own innocent people
Sending in a mighty, despised Egyptian army crushing a Revolt!
Underneath gloss they're fascists keeping their own Power base.
Mubarak's henchmen leading repression in the Battle of Camels.
Held in a Hypocritical cycle of Fear

'Imbaba Witness'
The Rage of Cairo's poor; Sent the Police to Shoot the people!
Crossing over the Nile ~"Aim to Kill" your Moslem brother,
your family sister, your Egyptian neighbor, terrorizing society.
Is this written in the Koran, how to Govern your people Abdel?
Ruthless crackdowns in Tunisia, Yemen, Bahrain, Syria, Libya!
Arab dictators' corruption, rigged elections torturing dissidents.
Filming Protests inspiring others to support humanity's cause!
Let's have it in the open, Blog it round the World, brave souls
using Internet to highlight the violence of Security force's thugs.
America got it wrong ~ Again supporting their own Dictators!
There's a Revolution at the Pyramids, toppling the old hierarchy.
Go and ask Khaled Saeed for evidence, exposing the Live fire....
Taken to the hated Ministry of the Interior for Interrogation!

Right Burks!
The Arab spring with a just cause to revolt for life but a dismal
British summer, hoodlums in disguise, Yobs in masks, want strife.
Nout else to do no higher ideals, stabbing pensioners with knives.
So pathetic, examples of cowardice confronting a Police State.
The Wealth and Power held and controlled by the richest 1%.
"It's yours now, the house and all the money"
"What shall we do with it?"
You are the Stooges!

Say No to Genocide!

"The few,1% keepin their low vibrational control over the many"
Your secret is safe with me ~"Kill them all and sort it out later!"
A Dishonorable Discharge for those who refused to participate.
Refusing to murder your mother father sister brother & children.
B52 atrocities attacking peasants with napalm, melting your skin.
500,000 U S soldiers deserted during Viet Nam War's projection.
Threw their Medals on the steps of Capital Hill in fierce Protest
at Agent Orange, fragmentation grenades from the Kitty Hawk!
Massacres at Mai Lai carried on into Afghanistan & Iraq today.
This fascism is gonna end in a Trail of Tears.

Prana Separation

'Dividing & Conquering' being taken over or taking over....
Plug into the Crystals ~ they'll get the intention resonating.
Invoking it and pushing it through.
Now cosmic frequencies ~ falling in that truth & beauty.
Empowerment being who you are.
A 5th Dimensional vibration ~ engaging in Your Reality.
How much do you want to Shine out in reflections?
Being a Medium in a blazing, amazing Spectrum!
Invoking that Presence ~ "Every breath we take"
Inspiration juice not back in the duality field.
'Having this and not having that'

'Turquoise Snapper'

Depending on that is Negative reflections ~
You are Truth ~ You can Trust, living it through.
Not going for delusion ~ In the old paradigm!
You almost stopped my heart,
when you fell from a star of Venus.
"What's goin' on inside your Mind-set?"
'WE WANT TO BE FREE'
Just remembering we are free.

Don't waste a minute

Can you change? Who is happy ~ Being creative, here & now.
Network par excellence ~ connection to a Conscious dimension
What is realistic to you? Meeting the right Guru! Crystal highs.
What do you want to do? Drop out ~ drop in, drop a drop.
Be spiritual, be a happy, peaceful human being, manifest Gold.
Where do you want to live with your gifts Sita?
Accepting life is changing beyond our Control or not.
Being enigmatic ~ be open, embracing all good forces.
Appeal to the Universe, ask the Stars, please the divine.
Recognition ~ Are you a Rebel, Pixie, are you a Player?
Allowing iridescent free spirits to exist ~ in the stream.

Rotating Wind Surfer & Spiral Shells

Bending air is Invisible ~ until it makes a movement.
Can't see it but can feel it; Nothing stops them blow.
'A freak of nature' put it down as an 'act of God'
Met an Italian experimentalist staring at the Mercury.
½ ton of air, less density on his atmospheric head!
Pressure dropping, the front didn't stop in Glasgow!
What to expect? Welcome to the Troposphere sailor.
Equatorial membrane accelerating around Earth, east > west.
Sensing signals, pulses, echoes, energies bouncing ~ revealing
speeds and directions, all circulating from the Sun's hot spot.
Powerful fortunes, knowing and controlling nature's patterns.
Navigating of elemental forces swirling through States of Chaos.
Following Polar insects on hurricanes from your tropical Island
where we collected hot cunilingus spice under a steaming Vortex.

Consummating fiery tips of shaved, red hot Irish Lilies

Flesh ~ Potion Sensual pleasure, resonating ~ radiant violets.
Envelopment of a resplendent, dripping, fecund sexual goddess.
She's painting a Love letter ~ reflections in her pink vulva pool.

Energetic Detective

"I'm following him in his frequency patterns ~"
"You think you lose energy, basically you fall in the Oneness"
We are it, we work through it, the Imprint of our individual ~
Kundalini with our own Creation shining out and being it.
Mother Earth is rebuilding herself as Gaia in the 5th dimension.
Enjoy the bliss of it All ~ Oneness

Crystal DC 10

Proper Indian Logic! "What is your good name?"
"I don't know who's bangin' at the door so hard?"
Constantly off his nut ~ definitely worth a squirt!
Ex STAtic bABYLONIAN ~ head's in the Trough.
Reptilian Republicans, 'Hallo to the Doctor!'
"It's not going to get any cheaper" ~ Boom Boom Free!

Strawberry Tips

"Keep talkin' to me Love tell me what you want ~"
'Avin a laugh with the people I'm workin' with!'
"We're gonna have it paletted right up!
Coming down the M5 ~ "Must have landed on a ley line
made me toes curl" ~ "The sky is full of Love"

Shot of Vodka!

Globalisation > 'Wealth makes Poverty'
Title track ~ "Throw in a Grenade or two!"
"Mara's name means delusion" Playing the B Side;
Is there any meaning to what we call Accidents?
Axis Mundi..."I had the butterflies all over me!"
"Life is what happens when you're busy making other plans"
"I never had a bad one" "You never had enough of them then!"
"I never like to wear a hat"~ "because that hat's wearing you"
"What's nice 'bout Crack?" Chimps & primates in Lockdown!
Your Mind altering substances!

<u>Qi Gong</u>
Small circle of Heaven ~
Field of the Pearl Inside.
Visualize ruby cosmic beams
snowing on the Himalayas.
Full of Chi in the sea
heated from the Sun.
Embracing the Prana

<u>Healthy Hard Rock!</u>
Spirit swimming in your heart ~ repetition.
'Letting reality play out ~ telling the story.
Sign of the times ~ they don't take rejection well!
Dark side of soulful flowers ~ the distorted message effect.
I know, realization that I am experiencing it all ~ no walls,
no virtual boundaries, no barricades in my brain processors'
Who has any ethics, don't let Business, greed Enslave you.
Is there anyone in touch with Truth? Hang in there and
keep on going through with Inspiration to Paradise Inside.
Lovely melody allowing conscious messages to get to the brain.
Bring it on!

<u>Sharing Inspiration</u>
'Don't let it bring you down it's only castles burning' Haiku.
Always Loved 'Crazy Horse & Searching for a Heart of Gold'
In keeping with the Holy Grail ~ a divine mission of humanity.
Whoopee "Give the tyrant a decent burial" Security for Babylon.
Who's digging for the Gold!? Prospecting in the River Psyche.
Still holding horrific blood lust; Time to stand up and REVOLT!
Sharpening your Spiritual weapons ~ take a Druid with you!
"Nothing left to lose" who said that? Janis Joplin or Boudicca?
Burning down the Imperial Temple full of collaborators!
"Thank You, Love the snake ~ Love your own Fear Inside"

Pond's White Beauty
What every Indian woman seems to aspire to be….
Ask the Corporate Psychologist, imitating Lakshmi!
Nearly dead and still full of fear; Oh fear is crap!
Who wants to be the Queen? Returning to Mars!
Changing my Insight ~ A Higher force in us.
Not your Ego Controlling everything ~
Then you Open ~ for it to come into your heart.

Thamsey Salmon
It was a tin of John West bobbing up Poison river.
Nobody told you to expect five finned GMO. Sharks!
Rusty cans of worms floating ~ reflections in the Pacific!
Muddy ground, surrounded by irradiated, corroded suits!

Herd Synchronicity
'Switching to a better World'
"I'M THE PARTY YOU'VE BEEN LOOKING FOR!"
"A lot of Sport is in the Mind" You don't know my trip!
"When they come they'll come for what you Love!"
US Collateral > "Shoot First Ask Questions later!"
Damage < "The wheels don't come off do they?"
"Swimming over the wall into Theta waves ~ with Creation
putting the Love download into the bubble and getting it…
Detox your Planet ~ if you believe in multi dimensionality.
Idea of a Phantasmagoria World ~ FLYING IN A DREAM.
Can't accept any Absolute diagnosis ~ I like Full Holistic.
What's your most + ve and most - ve experiences in Life?
Release all that negativity begin feeling All the Energy ~
The Integration of a beautiful person, new Inspiration.
"I don't heal anything ~ I just set up the conditions
for People to heal themselves"~ Simple & natural.
Give yourself that Gift ~

Sovereign's IOU!

"Bloody, ABSO's demonized kids on the street today.....
Yu wanna Kill people? ~ Put them in our Imperial Army!
Barking Mad ~ That's where they should go"
I lost my memory ~ I'm brainwashed enough!
Bullet in his Brain, body left in Cold storage in a fruit market!
& those Against Capitalist, Corporate greed; Health & Safety?
St Paul's Protest, closure costing £16,000/day in lost earnings!
Who are we in debt to? Nobody tells us that Primal fact; Why?
Who's holding the Power, who's Controlling our Governments?
Despotic 3 line whip of a rigid Party; No free democratic voting!
Might as well be in Pakistan, Kuwait, Saudi Arabia the big beasts!
It's all a Mirage, take it by the horns and tell it to "Fuck OFF!"
"Inshallah!" What's that really mean to you?

'Finite Resources?'

Ticket for Saudi women's Olympic synchronous swimming team!
Infinity Pool or your favela neighbours getting a cup of water.
Nuclear power Chandeliers in your mansion or Solar panels?
Royal Wedding budget or benefits for society's most deserving.
Forests for Export to IKEA or the habitat of 2/3rd of our Species?
"We're all in this together" is a Capitalist Government's mantra!
Bless, she's earning for her family to survive! Human Priorities!
In the subjugation of humans 'Ignorance is Bliss' who said that?

Prophet's wife in the Sun

Romancing 'A beauty beyond the senses' ~ a beauty of the Spirit.
The Luxury of Power, fragrance of Myrrh, any unrequited love?
Whose natural heart is so hardened? "You are No man's Slave!"
Gifts of the blessings of Life, tasting her as fresh Pomegranates.
She's voluptuous, bedecked in lace & Extraterrestrial influences.
Wanting the love of the fairest woman on Aphrodite's Planet ~
Deposing Sultans, enticing a Deity, becoming Myth, lost in time.

Master Mind Bender

In Mind when you're in the Ego ~ not you being in the moment.
Merging in no separation in the subconscious ~ celestial waves.
Self anaesthetizing ~"There can be no doubt of the Truth!"
Mind transmuted over the heart ~ Attracting you to me Cherie.
Invited to an orgy by a Maniac unfortunately I had to decline!
Exorcising all the Trauma no Micro Management here Please.
"I was raised with the flowers" ~ Will that star quality erode?
Attitude of Gratitude no more criticism, no speeches, no agendas.
Consciousness of life ~ happened like this; Nefertiti's piercings.
"Take her to the Chemist's to get some glasses"
You are it already, live yourself, to the Max.
Transmutation of our Core ~ Identity
We Identify to reflect life's experiences then let go…
The No Mind comes into ~ is the Cosmic emptiness.
The Refreshment of Life

Frequency Choice!

Having a democracy but not doing what the people want. Why?
Earth has many extremes of Life ~ Barbarity to a happy hippy.
Giving energy to water molecules spinning with Life force.
'He couldn't resist' Sacred ~ Imprint, is a tree is a tree is we.
What could be better than a woman being in Love and FREE?
Crystals' Information growing in the heart. Ask any Wahabi!
Performance Art ~ Begging! A nice landlord not a greedy man.
"Be nice to your Slaves" Angry synchronicity in the bluest sea.
You're projecting it from Inside yourself onto psychedelic reefs.
16 bars and the best of the drop, higher states of Consciousness.
What am I, what am I doing, what happened, what's goin' on?
She's the brightest side of the dark side of the funky Luna fairy.
Entering a 'Theatre of War' ~ or try Love Circuitry to reality?
Beyond Time ~ throwing Lotus petals to one another happily.
Permeating Satsang Shanti.

Captured Heroines

She was taken again down the corridor to le Salle des Tortures
in which there was a bath of cold water. The interrogator said,
"We have ways of making people like you talk." Ja mein Fuhrer!
She was pushed beneath the water until she nearly passed out ~
Today Water boarding is one of our Neo Gestapo's favorite Techniques!

Tulum Paradigm

I reflect the Confusion in the Chaos of the Zeitgeist
Diametrically Opposite to Cosmos' 'Divine Order' ~
In Mandala ~ Primordial energies Heaven and Earth.
Reflections of it from other holograms ~ the Unfolding.
You give it Peace and an Existence ~ Vital boundlessness.
Allowing it Space, allowing natural Synergies to be healing,
to be Integrated again ~ especially if you're not in the Mind.
Illusions of the Manifesting Matrix characterising all beingness.
Looking for symmetry ~ only in the now that you can understand.
That You Don't Have It In Your Mind ~ not in any past or future.
Externally created New Mind in a Computer ~ Stepping out of it
Into Consciousness even Cosmologists recognise that Program!
The Conquistadores didn't have the frequency with the Mayans.

"Their Magic was different"

'Life Is God' ~ "If you are Light there is no darkness."
"If you hide your light ~ can't clean your dusty crystal."
How you look out from your Inner source to a Milky Way.
Like a big juicy Sperm in Anjuna finding your way home ~
It's not Christian mate, Pagans and other savages do that!
"It's not a Problem, it's a Choice" The Ecstasy is Purer ~
All One ~ All in the now, dancing the dance, every moment.
She's a wobbler ~ going into it with the right heart.
Linked Consciously ~ Respecting the Freedom.
"They don't see the Spaceships in her eyes"

97

'Ma Femme Fatale'

Wake up from the hallucination "Never forget you're a Man!"
& she's a Queen of Lepidopterans flyin' on adrenalin & speed.
"Floating like an exotic butterfly stinging like a bubbly bee;
You're the Greatest, Full of Pep but don't fuck with me!"
My Boa's seducing your crested humming bird.

You know her tongue

Ordered into the Pasha's harem what do you say about slavery?
"Everything is as it should be" ~ Old enough to be corrupted!
Wars are made for the benefit of Kings ~ Are you Fearless?
"He's making some contact with this lovely, dependent bitch."
Why go there and get beaten! Go to see Guns & Roses instead.
Psyche Sky Baba, Guru's microphones in a Rock & Roll shop!
Went to see a Super Virtuality Show! An Assault on the senses.
Crazy on top, underneath it's calm ~"You're havin' a laugh!"
Loving festivals ~ lying in a Secret Garden, summers with you.
Everything to Uplift the Spirit ~ writing a Love Story in India!
I wish they could all be Khajuraho girls ~ dreaming the dream,
for a while there was only energy ~ Prepare to be burnt Sati!
Never about anyone else.

Dead in a Temple of Love

Cut down our DNA and enslaved us all. "I was reborn"
You gave yourself the experience by allowing.
It's all this Love ~ All of it.
Have to take it as Sacredly
What do you want to experience?
He was paid for rolling joints
in a Coffee shop in Amsterdam!
Beauty in the Transmutation.
Integration from Up and down.
Playing holistic gifts to the people.
Multi dimensional One with the Guru

"She's come to show you something!"
A lesson ~ I stay in the river in the free flow.
Same river ~ bouncing around with someone else!
"And Who said you could get out at the river bank?"
You gotta ride the waves ~ You gotta ride the whirlpools.
Monkey mind gotta grip of you ~ It's your movie playing.
"It's a jungle not a garden," too much alive in there!
Collective Individual, our decisions on all Levels.
Shock Loss & Grieving ~ It takes time to believe it!
You certainly manifested that one didn't you!?
Say what you want, not what you don't want.
No blocks, no resistances let her light up!
Feel it ~ Manifest it, hold it long enough for the Universe
to take a picture and give it to you ~ instantly, quick, click!
You already got it ~ something is pulsating in my Orgone.

In A Cellular Nutshell
"We're nothing but a blade of grass" Imitating Mother Earth
Programmed to do exactly what it's supposed to do Mr. Mimic.
A flower doesn't have a brain or eyes ~ Chemical Creationism.
"Nature's at it All the time!" forever blowing Organic bubbles
Whatever's down there is getting recycled and coming out ~
"It's about turning the Senses Inside and Seeing a light shine"
Your DNA code is reading what's goin' on ~ All the Programs!
It's why your Sperm is the most important thing in the Universe

Psychedelic Esoteric Scan
Whose Kevlar heart ~ not allowing any moment to unfold itself?
Takes patience for the 'Synchronicity' to appear in time ~ space
Allowing of the manifestation of the butterfly at your window.
We go inside the sensual ~ Protect rare & endangered species.
Dalai Lama, "It's my reincarnation, my rebirth ~ my business."
From dream visions appearing in Oracle Lake, Lhamo Lhatso.

What kind a hippie are you?
Illusion behind illusion behind Illusion behind Illusion ~ STOP!
Mary Croft, 'Creative Solutions' Strategic mortgage defaulting!
"If you can't do it then find someone who can!"
It is where you are in your own place ~
All this attachment to the worthless!
Driving like a Terrorist!

Super fluffy Firefly
They draw you into the light, shining out, giving fully Open ~
You're bringing your Old baggage. Now you've NEW patterns.
You recreated a new life; Just about how you talk to yourself.
Rejection, "Fuck off get back in your box!" Too old & fat cat!
Here to experience the Joy not to hold on; The hardest thing!
Then you connect inside.

Logos * Alchemy
We learn to Kill with our Mind! Human Predator in existence.
How to share Fire without instinct murdering each other for it?
We are the Fire ~ we burn Out. Get out of your own way ~
Make Space for it ~ to manifest or……………..

A Multi talented beauty from the wrong tribe
Female slave to the Ottomans maybe'll end up as an apprentice
Concubine! A brilliant sexual artist knows how to twist a Sultan.
Given to him as a gift to service his desires! A slave is property!
Sat on the Red Pyramid at Dahshur wondering what the fuck is
going on in this world ~ A magenta monkey walking into sight!
Light in the darkness coming from emotional & psychic planes.
Bringing in Abundance, holding the Earth, devoted to Venus ~
bringing laughter and the Sunshine into you ~
Conjuring joyful effervescence in your Soul.
Free Cosmic Orgasmic, you'll enjoy it more.

<u>'Press Gang Drama Club, Psycho babble'</u>
"I've mastered the Art of Appreciation"
Doing Mental Warrior Space training.
That's how Jedi's cream trifle is made.
Just whistlin' ~ a different frequency.
"I think I'm a Love junkie." Too much juice!
The word 'Weird' derives from 'Wisdom'
"Forget Outside the wall ~
NOW you're Inside the wall;
You have to get on with it!"

<u>With an Angel on Top</u>
All your Choclits lit up like a Clitmass tree!
The Ultra human dream, the Ultimate Love.
Know how to vibrate with it ~ in harmony.
Realising their Intuition of the Cycles ~
turning it on, seeing through the veils.
Accept the switch ~ Quantum Telepathy.
'New new' ~ Letting go of your knowledge
basking in an Ocean of Chaos ~ Infinite drops.
Try making heads or tails of it ~ Living it instead.

<u>Whose Soul's craving attention?</u>
Rainbow warrior, Sun worshipper, Freedom fighter at a Ceilidh.
My Sari of Dreams she weaved it from silk with Shiva moon man
Seductive Wild women, Ninja boots, big bag of Class A drugs!
Surrendering has nothing to do with giving up ~ it's Spiritual.
Trust to Trust going with free flow ~ guided by the inspiration.
Potency tuning its frequency, feeling it through natural Touch.
"I was Centred" in my sub conscious' vital stream of life force.
It happened that way, doesn't matter what you think you want.
Keep aware of equanimity, dhamma, whatever is, it's all Good.
Light workers raising vibrations of the Planet ~ unfolding Lotus
*from inside ~ Integration * go within or go without ~ All is Love*

You're Made to Feel Lucky
Multi dimensional ~ It's always changing, dust to dust, atoms....
Your Mind running you Or is that just an idea in your mind?
Poor sod what do you want, what will you accept?
All Subliminal Advertising, society telling you,
selling you a right 'Dirty Weekend' "Fuck You!"
She's a delight, full Rebel; "I'm being truthful"

On the line of Aphorism
Cooling down the Mind, cooling down the nerves
think about water ~ relaxing faces, lovely curves.
Passing on the compliments, the good vibe ~
"You look beautiful in that skin ~ tight thong"
Bollock naked, yu got the Gas fire on!?
'I'm living in my World'

Tripped Out!
"It's a Crime to run out of money, the sentence is Work"
'Keep away from them ~ Mad as a nylon brush!'
'That's when you bring the children into the house!'
It's all paid for ~ by All the in tune, like Minded people.
Healing on all kinds of Levels ~ losing all the judgmental...
bollocks someone could be Dictating that; You have a choice!
Not gone into molecules yet ~ in a stream of consciousness.
If you knew you wouldn't do it; Exploiting other people!
"My brother in law was full Psychedelic before Psy trance."
Eagles we notice all the time but don't See. Wow it's a vision!
I love the excitement of the Show & its creativity is Awesome.
Letting the sound bounce around your head ~ limitless.
Be sensitive Just observe your*self ~ where are you?
No Position to disconnect from ~ but it's all there.
Surge of DMT ~ Consciousness dancing ~ Soul Creation.
Expression not Illusion, it's already cohesive ~ happy.

<u>'Mind ~ the Gap'</u>
"Sacred ~ going into Space, Consciously.
Helping your Self ~ Facing Your true Self
Reflecting shifting ~ that's all I'm asking!"
We're all on the Verge ~ It's Common Sense.
Finally breaking the EGO ~ We all love to hug!
You will know that's why you're here ~ 'You can't not do it!'
Try some Complete detachment ~ from powerful enchantment.
In between the words, the states ~ is letting go of You.
Try something else ~ brand new subliminal discovery.
Being there on every Spiral of quantum holography
putting out those deflections, intentions, reflections.
It's not any Accessory ~ has to be right what you feel.
Helping me to Surrender ~ Your Gift to the Universe.
You are your only Judge ~ don't Identify with any of it.

<u>Caring Is Sharing***the Love***:)</u>
Tantric Energy Dreamy Space & All Loved Up, Effortlessly Aware.
"Connect to the Divine not some ET; Reptilian, Alien, projection"
There are none Superior to You as a child of the Cosmos.
'I AM THE SUPREME' ~ Form*less, Universal Infinity.
Get out of the Star wars; You are the highest species.
Being in the Spiritual not some Egoistic Pantomime.
"If you are a drop of the Ocean you are the Ocean"
The drop goes back into it all, you know you are this Ocean
but Your Mind wants you to disbelieve it ~ Self domination.
Have to stay out of its clutches, keep out of its way this Mirage.
It's all Illusions made of God, these Galaxies, Planets, UFO's!
Ultimately it's not there, it's his Maya he's playing hide & seek
with you and he's hiding where you'll never look ~ Inside You!
Soul within Super Soul. You gotta be in the right light frequency.
Abandon religions just surrender to All One ~ 'Il dolce far niente'
Love the Universe inside you***It's all alive there***
Feeling the Cosmic Ocean ~ Waves of existence

ABOUT SUNNY JETSUN

Inspired by the sixties Sunny started traveling the world in 1970. His spiritual journey on the hippie trail to India took him through San Francisco, Los Angeles, London, Amsterdam, Paris, Vancouver, Sidney, and Kathmandu to Varanasi. His arrival on the sub-continent was the beginning of writing autobiographical verses capturing his travel experiences, encounters with remarkable people and his quest for self-realization. Combining experimentation with drugs, sex, rock & roll, meditation, Love and life in general. Sunny started to open up to a multi-dimensional Universe. He lived the mantra, "Turn on, tune in, drop out" realising Mind's-illusions, inspired by deeper feelings of holistic nature, empathy*energy & Space.

Over four decades Sunny has written and published 28 books of poetry, created over one hundred paintings, traveled the World and considers his masterpiece to be his daughter. He has spent the past fifteen years in Goa, India inspired by the freedom to experience and idealism of human consciousness.

Sunny Jetsun books and art are available on the web at:

Website: www.sunnyjetsun.com
Facebook: www.facebook.com/sunnyjetsun
Amazon: www.amazon.com/author/sunnyjetsun
Smashwords: www.smashwords.com/profile/view/sunnyjetsun

www.ingramcontent.com/pod-product-compliance
Lightning Source LLC
Chambersburg PA
CBHW020509030426

42337CB00011B/293